FIRST CLASS
TRAVEL
on a Budget

HOW TO HACK YOUR CREDIT CARDS TO BOOK
INCREDIBLE TRIPS FOR LESS

FIRST CLASS TRAVEL
on a Budget

**ZACHARY
BURR ABEL**
CREATOR OF MONKEY MILES

PAGE STREET
PUBLISHING CO.

PAGE STREET
PUBLISHING CO.

First published in 2023 by
Page Street Publishing Co.
27 Congress Street, Suite 1511
Salem, MA 01970
www.pagestreetpublishing.com

Distributed by Macmillan, sales in Canada by The Canadian Manda Group.

27   26   25   24   23   1   2   3   4   5

ISBN-13: 978-1-64567-662-1

ISBN-10: 1-64567-662-5

Library of Congress Control Number: 2022946824

Cover and book design by Kylie Alexander for Page Street Publishing Co.

Printed and bound in the United States

Page Street Publishing protects our planet by donating to nonprofits like The Trustees, which focuses on local land conservation.

TO EVERYONE WHO HAS
READ THE BLOG OR
SUPPORTED ME ON
TIKTOK/INSTAGRAM,
THIS WOULD HAVE NEVER
HAPPENED WITHOUT
YOU. I HOPE THIS BOOK
AIDS YOU IN YOUR QUEST
TO MAKE YOUR BUCKET
LIST A REALITY.

TABLE OF CONTENTS

INTRODUCTION

Traveling has been one of the greatest joys of my life. I'm not only incredibly excited to share this joy with you, but, more importantly, I hope to inspire you to pursue your dreams. That little voice inside your head urging you to leap? Listen to it. It's there for a reason and nudging you to follow a path that will both challenge and fulfill you. Traveling has given me confidence, depth, perspective, and the ability to connect with people. It's made me feel alive, given me memories I share with those I love, and challenged me in ways I never could have imagined. I couldn't recommend it more.

By the time you finish reading this book, you'll not only understand how to build and improve your credit, properly evaluate a credit card, and engineer a wallet that aligns with your aspirations, but hopefully you will have learned how to think about these things, instead of what to think. My ambition is to equip you with the tools you'll need to intelligently navigate an ever-changing system and achieve your goals as they evolve over time.

Am I a certified financial adviser? Absolutely not. I do have a degree in finance. But what makes me most qualified to give advice is my everlasting, insatiable thirst to get a deal. I've even been described as fatally allergic to paying retail prices. I'm also willing to try things, and, despite not wanting to fail, I view failure as a means to achieving success. My failures have given me knowledge, and my ability to package that knowledge into fun, bite-sized, useful tips that resonate with millions of people has made me a go-to travel authority. Most of the successes I have had, the places I've visited, and the knowledge I've acquired are a result of this attitude toward failure. Hell, even writing this book is a grand experiment. If you'd told me years ago that I would become a published author, I'd never have believed you. Anything is possible.

What you'll begin to learn about me is that not only do I love to travel, I love to travel well. That was bred into me when I was young; my dad traveled a lot for work, and sometimes my mom and I were able to tag along to some incredible places. Those trips were a really big treat and an incredible opportunity for me to expand my horizons at a young age. I grew up in a small Midwestern town, and we didn't have any five-star hotels with croquet courts and frescoed ceilings. I'll never forget the time my dad had a conference in Florida. The three of us stayed at the Breakers in Palm Beach, and it was like walking through the pearly gates into heaven itself. Game over. I was done. I had learned what Egyptian cotton felt like, and I couldn't go back.

This book will help you develop the tools you need to carve out and create that same feeling on your future adventures. Whether it's a hotel, flight, or bucket list destination, it's one thing to do it, it's another thing to do it well—for a fraction of the cost.

You may think that I should have chosen to pursue a more traditional career path to finance my developing travel addiction. But in fact, my life has just forced me to find ever more inventive ways to stretch a dollar, and, honestly, I wouldn't have done it any differently.

After graduating with a degree in finance and international business from Washington University in St. Louis, I moved to New York City to pursue a career in acting. Yes, many of my friends became doctors, lawyers, and investment bankers while I passed crab cakes, sold outerwear at Bloomingdale's, and studied the Meisner method at T. Schreiber Studio in Manhattan.

Budgets were made, pennies were rubbed, and ends were always met.

A few years later, one thing led to another, and I was in Los Angeles acting full-time on a TV show. Robert Frost was right: I chose the path less traveled by and it *had* made all the difference. My dream was coming true. I was pursuing my passion and making great money, doors were flying open, and I began to travel more and more.

It just so happened that around this epoch, the credit card ecosystem massively transformed.

In 2009, Chase announced they were unveiling the Chase Sapphire Preferred card, and, through it, they debuted a rewards program intended to be the first true rival of American Express's Membership Rewards program. I became obsessed with points and miles and dipped my toe into the multiple credit card pond. I even managed to convince two of my friends to delve into the space for a big trip to Asia in 2012.

I was putting together a 17-night trip to Asia through Beijing, Singapore, Bangkok, and Kuala Lumpur, and pitched it to a couple of buddies. At the time, I was carrying an American Express Platinum card and thought we could leverage multiple deals through their Fine Hotels and Resorts program.

But while sitting in my car outside the LA Fitness on Hollywood Boulevard, I stumbled upon an ad for a new Hyatt credit card in a *Travel + Leisure* magazine. It blew my mind.

"Dave, Tyson, I have a sick deal I think we should do," I told my friends. "The Hyatt credit card is currently offering 2 free nights anywhere in the world after a single purchase, and the annual fee is just $75. Hyatt has some incredible properties in Asia. If we all got this card, we'd get 6 free nights for our trip."

We all pulled the trigger. The outcome? We did all 17 nights in five-star hotels, and, including flights and some incredible suites, it cost us about $2,000 a person. We couldn't believe the trip we took. We saw the Great Wall of China, ate at the hawker centers in Singapore, almost ran out of money in Kuala Lumpur, and did our best to re-create *The Hangover Part II* while in Bangkok. That trip around Asia was an integral step in my progression as a travel hacker.

Tyson Chambers, Dave Maurer, and I visting the Great Wall of China in 2012

I look back at it now and think, man, I left some great flights untapped and could have saved even more. One of the coolest parts of that trip was negotiating the best suite in the Peninsula Bangkok, the Peninsula Suite. We'd booked the hotel with American Express's Fine Hotels and Resorts program, and, upon arrival, we inquired about a discounted upgrade. Often, if you ask, hotels will dramatically discount prestigious suites for a reasonable amount. They gave us a discounted rate (we each paid $500 total for 3 nights), and, to this day, it was the most over-the-top experience of my life. We even had custom suit fittings in the living room. Needless to say, my passion for travel was fueled.

It wasn't all gumdrops and fairy tales though. Along with the excitement of this dream buddy trip, I also began to experience numbness in my foot. After leading a very active childhood and steadily working out as an adult, it was alarming. Over the next 2 years, I developed progressively worse back pain that got so bad I'd have spasms that would leave me unable to stand, curled up in a ball of pain on the floor. I was 34. After trying various noninvasive methods, I opted for surgery in November of 2014. It didn't fix the problem.

The doors that close are as important as the ones that open.

A three-month recovery turned into well over a year of chronic pain, and I was in desperate need of something positive to aid my mental health. Before long, I was spending 4 to 6 hours a day reading points and miles blogs. Sometimes more. I couldn't stop. Prior to having back surgery, I thought I knew quite a bit about credit and travel, but every door I opened led to another door. It became an obsession. Finally, my now wife, Elizabeth, as well as several friends (Daniella Giglio among them) strongly urged me to start a blog. I think they were really just tired of hearing my diatribes and thought a creative outlet would help me, but also them.

They were right.

One of the most incredible experiences was staying in the Peninsula Suite at the Peninsula Bangkok where we had custom suits fit.

Despite knowing absolutely zilch about starting a website, I knew I needed something to take my mind off the pain and unleash some of my creative energy. I thought to myself, what's my angle? How do I bring something different to the points and miles community? Then it hit me. I bought a domain on GoDaddy and voilà—I was a blogger with a stuffed monkey named Miles.

You were probably wondering about the monkey, huh?

At the time, I didn't know if I wanted my image to be out in front of a monkey named Miles—would people take me seriously in either field? I mean, who's going to listen to travel hacks from an actor on a teen drama? And would agents and managers representing me think I'd lost my acting commitment now that I was flying all around the world documenting my travels? I knew I could add value by bringing playfulness to a niche space that is effectively accounting and currency trading, and I thought having Miles on my site could make it fun. The reason so many people are frustrated with using points is because it can be downright boring to figure it all out. If I could make it a bit entertaining, I could really connect with people. But how would I do that?

I looked at my shelf and saw a cute stuffed monkey my parents had given me years ago. I was born in the year of the monkey, according to the Chinese zodiac, and have quite a bit of "monkey stuff" on my shelves as a result. I thought he was the perfect mascot for my site.

On May 7, 2015, I published my very first article: a review of Virgin Atlantic's Clubhouse at San Francisco Airport. My site was slow to load. I did everything wrong, and, after publishing a few more articles, my site flooded with spam comments and crashed. It was the first of many setbacks that ultimately educated me in ways money couldn't buy.

For the first year, I didn't make a single cent off my blog. But while I was building the website as a hobby, I also began hacking trips for my family and friends. One of my first big hacks was using points to fly my parents round trip to South Africa in first class on British Airways. The thrill of experiencing a safari with my family and my best friend, flying in business and first class, offsetting hotels with points, and taking pictures in front of sleeping lions really had me thinking. How do I keep doing this?

Then, a big door opened.

In the spring of 2016, I was on vacation (paid for with points) at the Hyatt Ziva in Puerto Vallarta with Elizabeth. We were lying on the beach when I got an email from BoardingArea—the very website that first piqued my interest years before—and now they wanted to partner with me! It was the validation I needed to keep going.

Once I joined BoardingArea, my site began to grow. Since then, I've published over 2,000 articles, planned celebrity trips, reviewed nearly every business class and first class in the world, and have gone on at least $1 million worth of trips with my family and friends to every continent. I've been to Tokyo, London, Beijing, and Bangkok just for the weekend; touched the pyramids in Egypt; swam the Great Barrier Reef; and climbed the Great Wall of China—and I've done all of it with points and miles.

But you know what really changed everything?

Things were going well, but I hadn't gotten that really big holy-mackerel-hold-onto-your-britches moment yet. I always thought perhaps I'd book another TV series and that exposure would pop my travel business to another level. In a weird twist of fate though, the thing that really changed everything for me was the pandemic.

If you were anywhere near the travel space at the start of the COVID-19 pandemic, your business was absolutely obliterated. I thought, whoever makes it through this with their head above water can really make some moves. As Warren Buffet said, "Be fearful when others are greedy and greedy when others are fearful."

In 2019, I stumbled upon Gary Vaynerchuk, known as GaryVee. He was constantly talking about how TikTok was going to be the biggest social media platform. Its users were growing exponentially, but its content wasn't.

Lightning struck.

Go all in when you have a distinct advantage and when there is very little competition.

I didn't lean into social media when I was on a TV show 10 years ago and always regretted not participating when I had a competitive advantage—a TV show! Now here I was listening to GaryVee plead his case that *this* was the time to go west my dear and drill for oil. That oil was the algorithm of TikTok and its rapidly growing network that everyone in the travel hacking space thought was for kids and dancing trends and represented a poor use of resources compared to Google and Facebook ads.

So I drilled. And I struck oil.

I've thought about this a lot. So many events in my life had to align for me to be walking on a random street in Hancock Park listening to GaryVee say just the right thing at just the right time when I was open to taking a risk and jumping off that digital cliff. It was divine orchestration, if you ask me.

My blog had been getting anywhere from 50,000 to 200,000 views a month, but TikTok put me in front of millions. You've heard the story about the 10-year overnight sensation? When it came to travel blogging, I was that story. TikTok gave me exposure, but the 2,000-plus articles I'd written over several years gave me authority. I knew my stuff, and publications like *Travel + Leisure* started referencing my tips and tricks to their readers.

OK, enough about me. This is about *you*. You're going to finish this book feeling empowered by the information you've learned that you can use to make educated decisions about your credit. You'll understand how credit is built and destroyed, the three types of credit cards, and how to incorporate them into your wallet strategy. My greatest hope, though, is that you finish this book feeling inspired. Inspired to help others conquer their credit, inspired to use your points to travel and experience different cultures, and, most important, inspired to pursue the pull of that little voice inside your head pleading with you to "take the road less traveled," because for me, it has made all the difference.

WHERE TO START

The golden rule of credit cards is to treat them the same way you would cash or debit. If you only charge what you can pay off in full, you'll enjoy all the benefits of your credit card without paying high interest rates. The horror stories of people racking up mountains of debt aren't to be dismissed, but if you approach credit cards with that one basic principle of only purchasing on them what you have the cash to cover, you'll make the system work for you. You'll have fraud protection, earn cash back or points for travel, and build your credit so that when it comes time to buy a house, you'll enjoy the best interest rates the market offers.

Credit is one of the most misunderstood and confusing aspects of adulthood and personal finance. It's very easy to ruin and can take years to repair. While people tend to understand the consequences of not paying their auto loan or mortgage, the way to properly use credit cards remains murky to most people.

I've had a lot of interactions on social media with people who think the sheer fact of having a credit card means you're paying exorbitant interest and are saddled with heaps of debt. Having a credit card certainly requires self-discipline and budgeting, but the idea that using a credit card is financially irresponsible couldn't be further from the truth. In fact, it's the exact opposite if you're using them as I do: letting someone else pay you to borrow their money.

Pretty awesome, right?

The points earned from credit cards have made it possible for me and my family to travel in ways we never imagined. Like when my dad and I surprised my mom with an around-the-world trip in business class and first class for her 75th birthday. Over the course of 24 nights, we only stayed in four- and five-star hotels and traveled to the Great Wall of China, Bali, Singapore, Dubai, Abu Dhabi, and the South of France, where we visited the Molinard factory which makes the perfume my mom has worn for 50 years. The retail cost of the trip would have been $125,000. We used points and spent $5,000 total.

Here's a picture of us in our suite on Singapore Airlines, which we flew from Beijing to Singapore. Yes, this is a plane. Yes, that entire section converts into a massive bed that my parents slept in. Yes, they would kill me if I put that picture here instead of this one :).

So where do we start? Well, before we dive into the wild world of travel hacking, let's address some super basic principles that will help lay the groundwork for what we'll be discussing.

- **Credit Line:** This is the maximum amount of debt a lender has determined they can lend you. If it's associated with a credit card, it's the total amount you can charge to that card.

- **Interest Rate:** This is the interest rate you will pay on your outstanding debt. Usually this is compounded annually, and if it's for a credit card, you'll only pay interest on the amount you don't pay in full each month.

- **Minimum Payment:** This is the bare minimum you can pay without having a missed payment reported to a credit bureau. Interest will be charged on the difference between your minimum payment and the total balance.

- **Statement Balance:** This is the amount of money you owe for charges made during a specific period of time. If you don't pay the statement balance in full, it will be added to your total balance.

- **Total Balance:** This is the total amount of charges you've incurred on a line of credit that hasn't been paid off, including interest, late fees, etc.

- **Total Available Credit:** This is your total credit line minus the total balance owed.

- **Credit Card vs. Charge Card:** A credit card has a line of credit associated with it that can be paid over time while accruing interest on the outstanding debt. A charge card needs to be paid in full every month.

- **Annual Fee:** This is the fee the bank charges you every year to keep a credit card.

- **Late Fee:** If you don't make the minimum payment by your due date, the bank will charge you a fee for missing that payment. If this lapses by more than 30 days, they could report it to a credit bureau.

Above all else, you want to adhere to these three basic credit card principles:

1. Always pay off the balance in full and on time.
2. Use credit cards that provide benefits that are more valuable than your annual fee.
3. Keep credit cards that earn the right kind of points to achieve your goals, whether they are cash back or travel based.

I usually have between 20 and 30 credit cards at any given time, and that doesn't include what my wife has! I continually come back to those three basic principles. As long as I'm paying a card off in full, extracting more value from it than what I'm paying to keep it, and earning points on it to get me closer to my goals, I'll keep it. I don't care if it costs $695 a year and I get $696 of value, I consider it a deal. If a card stops providing benefits and is no longer valuable to me, well, that's when things start to get interesting.

There are all sorts of ways to utilize the credit system to your benefit, and that's what I'm here to help you better understand. Let's take the next step by cracking the code on your credit report and credit score. This will give you the building blocks you'll need to master the system and achieve your goals.

CRACKING THE CODE ON YOUR CREDIT

Twenty years ago, during my junior year of college, I successfully opened a Fidelity brokerage account and invested the little amount of money I had in various stocks and ETFs (exchange traded funds). I was a finance major, flirting with a banking career, and, while this may not seem like such a feat in today's Wall Street bets/cryptocurrency world, back then, without Wi-Fi, I was very proud to have a Fidelity brokerage account.

Pride ultimately is what undermined my credit score. That Fidelity brokerage account had the ability to opt into a Fidelity American Express Gold card (similar to what Charles Schwab has today with Amex cards). I went to Washington University in St. Louis, and, let me tell you, a lot of the kids flashed credit cards linked to their parents' accounts as if they wielded the power of that credit line themselves. Prior to opening my Fidelity account, I had a simple blue Chase credit card that I always felt insecure using alongside my friends' fancier cards. So silly, but it's the truth. My pride got the best of me, and I got a Fidelity-branded Amex Gold card.

After college, I moved to NYC to pursue acting, and Fidelity offered to upgrade my Gold card to the illustrious Platinum card—again branded with a Fidelity emblem—and I couldn't believe it. Rumor had it, in 2003, the Platinum card required a $100,000 income, which, as a struggling actor working in the Bloomingdale's outerwear section, I certainly did not have. Every time I pulled it out to pay for something, I felt that prestige effect. Again, so silly.

I was doing the exact opposite of what I now advocate on MonkeyMiles.com, on social media, and again in this book. Learn from my mistakes. You need to build a wallet that serves your goals, and, in order to do that, you need to understand how the credit system works so you can use it to your advantage.

Cards like the Amex Platinum certainly carry a lot of prestige, but if you're just building your credit, there are cards that help you a lot more. It wasn't all downsides. My Fidelity Amex Platinum got me a discounted Equinox membership, which I loved (again, a perk in 2022), and whenever I flew out of LaGuardia Airport, I could pop into the Delta lounge simply by flashing my Amex Plat. While I was extracting value, I was actually missing out on really building my credit.

Why? Those Fidelity Amex cards didn't have any credit lines associated with them. Instead, they deducted money from the cash reserves of my Fidelity account, much like a debit card, and unbeknownst to me, I was sacrificing building my credit to artificially boost my ego.

When I graduated from Washington University, it was one of the top 15 schools in the country, and I held a degree in finance. I could speak at length about the Black-Scholes model, whether you should employ FIFO (first in, first out) or LIFO (last in, first out) accounting, but did I learn about how my credit score was derived? Absolutely not.

When you're starting out and looking to build your credit profile, it's imperative that you use credit cards that issue you a line of credit. Paying this line off in full every month shows that you pay back your debts. As you become more responsible, proving you pay on time and in full, more institutions will issue you credit to use, and your score will continue to strengthen.

Why? This is one of the most misunderstood aspects of credit formation.

The more credit you have at your disposal that you don't use, the better your score will be. I know this probably sounds completely counterintuitive, but it's a fact. The old wives' tale that you'll ruin your credit if you have more than one credit card is a lie. Sorry, old wives.

Yes, this may be surprising to hear, but having just one credit card actually could be suppressing your score. You pay on time, in full, but your credit score is stuck in the mid to low 700s. Why? A big reason could be that you're using too much of your allotted credit and possess only a single trade line. Little did I know that using my Fidelity Amex Platinum card was keeping my score lower than it could have been.

I mentioned I had another card in my wallet. It was one that my parents had been cosigners on when I was 18 to help build my credit. It was from Chase, pale blue, and looked like I was just hoping whatever I was charging would get approved. I always used that card when my

Fidelity account was fully invested and didn't have any cash reserves to cover my Amex bills. Had I just kept using that simple Chase card, it would have done more for my credit score, and my long-term ability to travel hack, than the Amex Platinum that was linked to my Fidelity account. Why?

To fully understand, you need to know how your credit score is built, how to secure it, and ultimately how to weaponize it to travel the world and score the lowest interest rates when you buy your dream home. Let's get into the basics of a credit report, how your credit score is formulated, and why I would have been better off with a simple "slip it under the check and don't make eye contact" card instead of my Fidelity "I could drive a Lambo and live in South Hampton" card.

UNDERSTANDING YOUR CREDIT REPORT AND CREDIT SCORE

File this under things they should have taught you in school. Why on earth is personal finance not one of the main focuses in school? It's so disappointing to consistently speak to people who have stumbled into the honey pot of credit problems simply because they don't understand the basics of credit.

Let's fix that right here and now.

Every person has a credit report and a credit score. They are different, although related, and understanding what each one is, and how they are used, can save you an enormous amount of money.

OK, so what's a credit report?
Your credit report is very different from your credit score (which we'll cover later) and includes an extensive accounting of all the times you've used credit over the past 7 to 10 years. There are three credit reporting bureaus that keep a relatively similar accounting of your credit history. Each bureau may have slightly different information, so it's important to keep an eye on all three of them.

The three bureaus that provide those reports are:

- Equifax
- TransUnion
- Experian

Each bureau has an aggregate of all the information that has been reported by creditors, and that is called your credit report. You're entitled to get a copy of your credit report from each bureau every year—currently the best place to get it is annualcreditreport.com.

As I mentioned, each of these bureaus may have a slightly different set of information, since there aren't any laws that require creditors to report information to any, or all, of the bureaus.

For instance, if you live in New York and apply for a credit card, the bank may use your Experian credit report, but that same bank may use TransUnion if you live in California. That's why it's good to get a report from each bureau every year so you can assess it for errors, fraud, or, as you'll learn from my mistake, missed bills that end up in collections.

What information is in a credit report?

Your report is a full accounting of your credit history and includes important information that ultimately decides how your credit score is formed. If you're just starting out with credit, your report may be fewer than 20 pages long. On average, if over the past 10 years you've opened a few credit cards, leased a car, and bought a home, I'd guess you'll end up with a credit report that's 30 to 40 pages long.

I've had a lot of trade lines, especially because I open a lot of credit cards, and when I recently received my batch of free credit reports, each bureau had 70 to 80 pages of information on me relating to the following items:

Information used to identify who you are

- Past addresses, Social Security number, date of birth, etc.

Credit account information

- The credit you have or have had in the past, such as credit cards, mortgages, student loans, auto loans, and apartment leases

A record of your credit inquiries

- Hard inquiries, when you open a new line of credit, and a hard pull is completed and reported to credit bureaus
- Soft inquiries, when you check your credit score, or your current creditors take a peek at your report

Bankruptcy

- Chapter 7, which stays on your report for 10 years, requires no repayment of loans upon court approval

- Chapter 13, which stays on your report for 7 years, requires repayment of loans with a repayment plan

Collections

- You failed to pay a bill and currently have a collection agency seeking payment

- You successfully disputed a collection, which takes 7 years to be removed from your report

All of this information is collected to build a profile of your past behavior so that creditors can forecast how you'll behave if and when they lend you money. It's a lot of information to sort through. Can you imagine going through all 80-plus pages of my credit report? It'd take a lender all day, copious amounts of coffee, and perhaps some experimental artificial intelligence to come to a conclusion about whether I qualify or not. So, decades ago, the fine people at the Fair Isaac Corporation developed an algorithm, and the FICO score was created.

If I have my credit report, why do I need a credit score?

You need a credit score simply . . . to make things easier.

The Fair Isaac Corporation, more commonly known as FICO, figured out how to condense all the information in your credit report into a snapshot. Yes, all of that information, your entire credit history, is reduced to a single score, and that score impacts most anything you'll end up doing that involves borrowing money.

A competitor to FICO popped up in 2006 called VantageScore, but their purpose is the same: They quickly and easily give lenders a snapshot of your credit history so they have the ability to assess how risky you are to them as a borrower.

Should I trust FICO or VantageScore?

Both FICO and VantageScore give you an idea of where you stand, but approximately 90 percent of all lenders will use your FICO score to determine whether they will lend to you, and what interest you'll pay on that borrowed money.

For that reason alone, while you may get a VantageScore credit score from your credit card company or bank, for our purposes, we're only going to examine FICO, since it's what ultimately matters the most when it comes time to borrow. My VantageScore credit score has always been pretty close to my FICO score, but I've seen people's scores that have been off by 40 or even 50 points. That's a big shock when you think you have great credit and apply for a loan only to find out your FICO score is much lower.

If, in the future, lenders start to overwhelmingly use VantageScore credit scores, I'll pivot. But for the time being, FICO is what's used most, so that's where we will focus our energy.

Are there different types of FICO credit scores?

FICO has different scores and algorithms for different types of credit, and those algos continue to evolve (yes, I say "algos" because I'm cool, in case you were wondering). If you're applying for a loan for a car or a home, they may tweak the algorithm and weigh things like new accounts more heavily than if you're applying for a credit card. Same goes for a personal line of credit.

We're focusing on credit cards in this book, and the latest FICO score that reflects how you look to credit card lenders is the FICO 10. You may have access to FICO 8, FICO 9, and FICO 10, and all of those would be good indicators of what a credit card lender would see when they pull your score.

I've found the easiest place to get a free FICO score is via Experian, one of the major credit bureaus. They offer a suite of services, like credit boosting and monitoring, that you'd need to pay for, but if you're simply looking for a free FICO score, they offer that as well. Additionally, if you're looking at leasing a car or getting a personal loan or mortgage, they have tools to acquire the FICO scores correlated to those credit lines.

What's a good FICO score?

You want a great FICO score, and you'll be happy to hear it has nothing to do with how much money you make. It's all about how you use the credit that is given to you. You could be making $50,000 a year and have a credit score far higher than someone making $250,000. That's the American dream right there!

FICO scores range from 300 to 850, and this is how FICO ranks their scores:

- 300 to 579: Very Poor to Poor
  - » You will get very high interest rates and find it next to impossible to get credit cards.
- 580 to 669: Poor to Fair
  - » At the low end of this range, you will be given subprime rates.
- 670 to 739: Acceptable to Good
  - » Lenders will more or less extend credit to you, but your rates won't be the best.
- 740 to 799: Very Good
  - » Anything over 740 to 750 means you're getting the best rates available.
- 800 to 850: Excellent
  - » You won't be getting better rates than those with 750 scores, but you can brag to your friends.

The higher your score, the higher the odds you will repay all of your debts. The lower your score, the higher the odds you will default and not repay. This is how lenders view you and why there is an inverse relationship between interest rates and credit scores. As your risk goes up, so does the payment to the lender to justify tolerating that risk to lend you money.

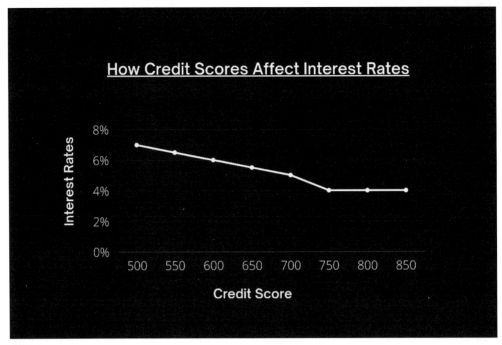

How Credit Scores Affect Interest Rates

The higher your credit score is, the lower your interest rates will be on a loan.

This chart shows the correlation between interest rates and credit scores. The numbers are arbitrary, but you can see that once your score gets above the 740 to 760 range, you don't see any real reduction in interest rates. At this level, you're considered to have top-tier credit, and the risk associated with lending money to you is very, very low. As I mentioned, anything above 750 just gives you bragging rights.

How is my FICO score calculated?
Your FICO score is calculated using five factors, and each has a different impact on your credit score. The failure to understand these differences has led many people to have misconceptions about what actually improves and hurts their credit score.

Let's take a look at each of these factors, how they impact your score, and ultimately why I'm able to keep over 20 credit cards and have top-tier credit (bragging rights included).

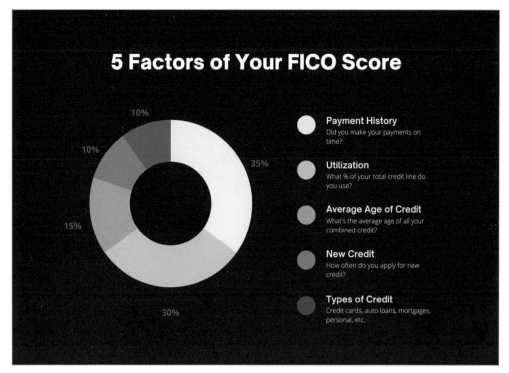

5 Factors of Your FICO Score

10%

10%

35%

15%

30%

Payment History
Did you make your payments on time?

Utilization
What % of your total credit line do you use?

Average Age of Credit
What's the average age of all your combined credit?

New Credit
How often do you apply for new credit?

Types of Credit
Credit cards, auto loans, mortgages, personal, etc.

As you can see, payment history and utilization are the biggest pieces of the pie and, thus, the most important.

The five factors of your FICO credit score

Here's a breakdown of the different factors that we'll dig into in more detail:

Your payment history makes up 35 percent.

• Also known as on-time payments

Your utilization makes up 30 percent.

• Also known as amounts owed or credit usage

Your average age of credit makes up 15 percent.

• Also known as length of credit history

Your new credit makes up 10 percent.

• Also known as new lines of credit or new inquiries

Your types of credit make up 10 percent.

• Also known as credit mix or lines of credit

1. The Most Important Factor: Payment History (35 percent)

Thirty-five percent of your FICO score is derived from how often you pay your bills on time, and whether or not any of them have ever been sent to collections. That doesn't mean you have to pay off all your debts in full, but when a payment is due, you make it. If this number isn't 100 percent on time, you're going to pay the price with a major ding to your credit score. If you've heard the saying, "Always late, but worth the wait," it doesn't apply here :).

If you fail to make a payment on the due date, there is a grace period. Ordinarily, the grace period is 30 days past your due date. After that? A lender can send you to collections. Often, the credit card companies assess a late fee and interest if you don't make a payment but won't send you to collections after 30 days. Anecdotally, 90 days is the cutoff, but it's possible the bank will pull the trigger sooner.

Lemme tell you a quick story about how I unknowingly ruined my credit in my early 20s and didn't know about it for a couple of years. This was way before I became obsessed with travel hacking and only kept a couple of credit cards in my wallet. Hopefully, this is a cautionary tale that will allow you to learn vicariously through my mistake, so you don't repeat it.

In the summer of 2005, after roughly 2 years in NYC, I landed acting representation in Los Angeles. I made plans to move, and just before I did, I got a sinus infection. Thankfully, I had medical insurance, so I visited a doctor nearby and was given some antibiotics and told my insurance would be billed.

"How about my copay?" I asked.

"A bill will be mailed to you for your copay and anything your insurance doesn't cover," I was told. I put my fancy Fidelity Amex Platinum away and skipped back to my apartment on 61st and Lex.

A few days later, I packed up a U-Haul and began my move to LA. At the time, my two roommates were planning on staying in the apartment we all rented, but a couple of months later, they ended up leaving as well. I had remembered to change any utilities under my name and my credit card mailing address, and I presumed they would send me any mail that slipped through the cracks. My fatal error: I never registered a forwarding address with the post office.

Can you see where this is going?

Two years later, I walked into a Jeep dealership on La Brea to inquire about leasing a Grand Cherokee. They ran my credit. Remember, I'd had a credit card since I was 18, and I had always paid my credit card bills off in full and on time (yes, I am a Virgo), so I was sitting there 7 years later waiting to hear the good news: "Sir, you have great credit, and we can offer you a really competitive interest rate on your loan or lease."

Imagine my shock when I heard: "Sir, we ran your credit, and your score is in the 650s. This is what we can offer you for a lease payment based on that score."

What? The world slowed, *SSSSSIIIIIXXXXX FFFFFIIIIIFFFFFTTTTTYYYYY*. I was apoplectic and in complete denial. They gave me a copy of my credit report, and it was right there—I had a bill that went to collections.

At first, I thought it was surely a mistake. How was this even possible? I'd never missed a rent payment, credit card bill payment, nothing (as I said, I'm a Virgo). Once my vision returned, I told the salesman I'd have to look into this and get back to them.

When I phoned the collection agency, I was informed that a bill from a medical office in NYC had been sent to collections for nonpayment after 180 days. The bill? It was for $5. My copay was a measly $5, and my naive self never filled out paperwork for mail forwarding, which meant I never received that copay bill, and the cost of a latte shattered my credit. I paid the $30 (collection agencies add on some hefty fees), ironically with my trusty pale blue Chase credit card, and almost vomited. That one mistake ruined years of hard work.

The size of the unpaid debt doesn't matter one bit. Even the littlest of unpaid balances can send you to collections and significantly wound your credit score.

"Zach, a similar thing happened to me. I had a medical bill go to collections, resolved it, but it's still hanging around. How long until it's removed?"

Ordinarily, it would take 7 years to see collections wind off your credit report. However . . .

As of July 1, 2022, the three major credit agencies—Equifax, Experian, and TransUnion—now remove paid medical debts from credit reports. If you're affected by this, you should see an immediate boost to your score. In addition to removing paid medical debt, unpaid medical debt won't show up until 12 months have passed (mine went to collections at the 6-month mark). This will give people longer to negotiate a payment plan with the medical provider owed payment. Also, starting in 2023, the big three will cease to include medical debt under $500 in credit reporting.

While measures are being taken to help alleviate the burden of medical debt, the lesson remains the same. It doesn't matter the size of the unpaid balance you have; if you don't pay it on time, or leave it unpaid altogether, your credit will take a serious hit.

"Zach, does payment history mean paid in full?"

No, paid in full just means that when your payment is due, you make a payment. With credit cards, I advocate paying the balance off in full every month. The interest associated with credit cards is egregiously high and never warrants carrying a balance. However, if you pay what is due by the due date, your payment will be recorded, and your payment history will remain 100 percent.

The same goes for homeowners' association dues, mortgages, auto loans, leases, etc. As long as you are paying the minimum payment negotiated for the installment, your payment history will be 100 percent.

Here are a few tips to help you keep a 100 percent on-time payment history:

- Use personal finance apps like Prism, BillMinder, or Mint to set reminders for bill payment.
- Set monthly recurring reminders on your smartphone calendar for each bill.
- Many credit cards will allow you to set due dates; align them all to fall on the same day so you remember to pay them.
- Sign up for autopayment with email confirmation.

2. The Easiest Way to Boost Your Credit Score: Credit Usage/Utilization (30 percent)

This factor represents a whopping 30 percent of your FICO score and is by far the most misunderstood aspect of your credit score. If you're paying your bills on time, in full, and are wondering why your score isn't improving, it may be because of your credit usage or credit utilization. This is ultimately why it would have served my credit score to use my pale blue Chase card instead of my fancy Amex Platinum card. Let's unpack this.

Credit usage or utilization is calculated like this:

$$\frac{\textit{How much credit you are using}}{\textit{The total amount of credit available to you}}$$

Utilization is the main reason why I can keep over 20 credit cards and maintain a top-tier credit score. Contrary to a common misconception, having a lot of credit cards doesn't injure your credit, having a high utilization is what kills your score. Even if you're paying all your bills on time, if you're using a high percentage of the credit allocated to you, your credit score will take a hit.

Ideally, if you're looking to get your score into that coveted 750-plus area, you'll need a single-digit credit usage rate. Let's unpack how you can achieve this and earn a lot more credit card points.

Let's use me as an example from when I lived in NYC. I had two credit cards: One was a fancy Fidelity Amex Platinum card that had no credit line and the other was my pale blue Chase card that had roughly a $5,000 credit line. On average, I probably charged anywhere from $1,500 to $2,000 a month in total on my credit cards. I paid my bills off in full and on time, everything else on my credit report was solid, but my score hovered below that 740 to 760 range we all want to be above.

Why?

The most glaringly obvious thing to me now was my credit usage number. I was using $1,500 to $2,000 out of the $5,000 I had available to me. That was a whopping 35 to 40 percent of my total credit line, and for lenders, that's a potential red flag that could mean trouble.

Doesn't make sense, right? I paid all my bills in full and on time, plus I was doing what I thought I was supposed to do. So what could I have done to improve my score?

Solution #1: I could have stopped using my Amex Platinum and put all my expenses on the Chase card that had a credit limit. After a few months of using $1,500 to $2,000 of that line, I could have contacted the bank and requested a credit line increase. They'd look at my history with the bank and see that my account was nearly 7 years old and was always paid on time and in full. Let's say they agreed to double my limit to $10,000. Within a couple of months, I'd guess that my credit score would have improved. My utilization would have dropped below 20 percent, which is still not ideal, but well below the warning zone I was in before.

Some banks will do this without a hard inquiry, meaning they do a soft pull, and there aren't any dings to your credit score. Unfortunately, others will do a hard pull to extend a deeper line of credit. Hard pulls usually drop your score anywhere from 3 to 10 points, though your score recovers within 6 to 12 weeks. If you're going to potentially have a hard pull, I'd recommend considering Solution #2. A bank will tell you if they are going to conduct a hard pull, but the quickest way to find out is to do a quick search online.

Solution #2: We'll go into further detail about this in the section that explains the fourth factor of credit, new inquiries, but as I mentioned before, a hard pull, or inquiry, doesn't have that big of an impact on your score. If you're going to have a hard inquiry, though, I believe you should get something in return.

I could have applied for a new credit card that was offering a sign-up bonus. I'd argue it's better to do this with a new bank since most banks will only extend you a certain amount of credit based on your income. Let's say I made $60,000 when I had my Chase card. Chase may have only issued me $6,000 credit in total, but a new bank might give me another $5,000 as a new client.

Meaning, often you can deepen your overall credit lines more by opening a card with a new bank rather than requesting a credit line increase. This would also establish a credit history for me with a new bank, which certainly isn't a bad thing.

So let's say I get approved for a new card with a $5,000 line of credit. This would ultimately have the same effect on my credit as increasing the line on my existing card—it deepens my overall credit line across all lenders while my spending remains the same. The fraction of credit that I use goes down and thus reduces my utilization number. The added benefit here is that I could get a great sign-up bonus, which could have put me closer to that aspirational trip on my bucket list. This is often the case these days compared to 20 years ago when sign-up bonuses were a fraction of what they are today.

Over time, I would do a combination of Solutions #1 and #2, either requesting deeper lines of credit on established lines, or adding another card to deepen my total available credit. The thing I wouldn't do is increase my expenses. The goal would be this:

$$\frac{Spend < \$2,000 \ a \ month}{Available \ credit > \$20,000 \ total}$$

If I started to make more money and spend more, I'd seek deeper lines of credit to ensure that my utilization rate would stay under 10 percent to give me the best odds of attaining that top-tier credit goal.

"Zach, should I pay my bill off before the due date?"

This is something that is widely debated and can sometimes open the door to increased scrutiny over what's called credit cycling. If you have a really low credit line, you may be maxing out your card before the monthly statement closes. If you max out your card, pay off that balance before the statement closes, and then start charging again, you may raise some eyebrows at your bank. Why? This is a practice used by people who launder money, so you could inadvertently trigger your bank's warning system for an AML violation—an anti-money laundering violation.

This is usually a problem when your total charges are more than your credit limit. One thing you could do is to pay off part of your balance before your statement closes. Why? The amount of credit you use monthly isn't reported throughout the month, it's reported when the statement closes. So if you can lower the amount reported to the bureau, you can lower your utilization.

Here's an example:

I have a $5,000 limit on my Chase card and I charge $2,000. My statement closes on March 31, but instead of waiting for the statement to close, I make a $1,600 payment on March 25. It shows up on my account, and my statement closes with just a $400 balance on a $5,000 line of credit, which is below 10 percent utilization.

Here are a few tips to help you minimize your utilization:

- Aim for under 10 percent utilization even though "experts" say 30 percent.
- Ahead of your statement closing, pay down part of your credit line.
- After 6 months to a year, request a credit line increase.
- Add new lines of credit to help deepen your overall credit.

3. Average Age of Credit (15 percent)
The golden rule for conquering this factor—don't close your oldest account.

This sounds like a relatively simple factor. You can easily check when an account was created, calculate its age, and repeat the process for all your accounts. If you have four accounts on your credit report that have been open for 15 years, 8 years, 7 years, and 2 years, you'd have a total of 32 years of credit. Divide that by four cards, and your credit has an average age of 8 years.

This is why it's imperative that you keep your oldest accounts open. If you don't want to pay an annual fee, see if the lender will downgrade the account to a no-fee version. Keeping that old card open, even if you only use it once a year for a cup of coffee, will help boost your average age of credit.

"Zach, you said that this is a relatively simple factor, what am I missing?"

Remember when we talked about there being various FICO scores? Well, a lot of lenders still use the FICO 8 (there have been updated versions since, namely FICO 9 and FICO 10), and FICO 8 includes closed accounts in your average age. Closed accounts are included in a FICO 8 until they fall off your report (typically after 10 years of being closed). If your closed card had any delinquencies or unpaid balances, it will take 7 years for that information to be removed from your credit report, but the FICO 8 will continue to use the age of that account to calculate your score. This is a big difference between FICO 8 and the newer FICO versions as well as VantageScore, which doesn't include closed accounts in its calculation of average age. When I look up my FICO 8 score, it tells me that my average age is almost 9 years, while VantageScore tells me my average age is 7.5 years. Clearly, I have some closed accounts that were opened over 10 years ago, but it hasn't been 10 years since they were closed.

"Zach, what's the goal for average age of credit?"

If you're really trying to rank as excellent, the closer you are to having an average age of 10 years, the better. But I've never had an average age over 10 years, with 5 to 8 years being where I usually land, yet I consistently have an 800-plus FICO score.

There's also the authorized user trick. I have an account that has over 42 years of credit history. How is that possible when I'm only 41? Well, I'm an authorized user on one of my mom's cards. One of the easiest ways to add length to your credit history is to become an authorized user on someone else's account that has a really long history (no judgment on your age, Mom!). Not every bank will report an authorized user to a credit report, but a lot do, and it's an easy way to boost your average age of credit when your profile is young and slim (like me).

Here are some tips for keeping your average age of credit healthy:

• Never close your oldest card.

• Downgrade cards to no-annual-fee versions to keep the credit lines open and the clock running on their age.

• Become an authorized user on a family member's old account to increase your average age.

4. New Credit or New Inquiries (10 percent)

I regularly get comments from people who believe that opening multiple credit cards in a year ruins your credit. Here's the truth. It doesn't help your credit score, but opening five-plus credit cards a year over the last decade has done little long-term damage to my score. In fact, I'd argue it's had no negative impact. Though the impact can be different depending on where you are in your credit journey.

What I've found is that normally you will incur a 3- to 10-point hit to your credit score in the short term. Within 6 to 12 weeks, your score will usually recover fully, and, oftentimes if you're adding a new line of credit, the long-term effect is positive. Why? New credit or credit inquiries only account for 10 percent of your FICO score, whereas utilization has a 30 percent impact. If the credit you're adding is helping to deepen your available credit, your utilization will go down, and this helps to improve your score. Usually, the improvement outweighs the 3- to 10-point hit.

"Zach, what counts as an inquiry?"

Any time there is a hard pull on your credit report, it counts as an inquiry. A hard pull may be done for a new apartment, mobile line, utilities for your house, cable/Internet account, or credit card.

"Zach, do soft pulls count as an inquiry?"

Nope. In fact, soft pulls are done any time you check your own credit score, so don't worry about doing it as often as you want to. Most lenders you do business with will conduct routine soft pulls to see how you continue to look as a borrower.

"Zach, does it affect my credit if I'm not approved?"

Absolutely. If you aren't approved for a card, you'll still get the ding on your score. It doesn't matter whether you add a new line of credit or not, the inquiry will drop your score regardless.

"Zach, how long do those new inquiries stay on my report?"

As I mentioned before, it usually takes 6 to 12 weeks to see your score recover, but the inquiry itself will stay on your report for 2 years.

"Zach, how often should I apply for a new card?"

This is a very personal decision, and everyone's goals and strategy are completely different. Here is how I would generally approach things:

- **New Credit Profile:** If you're just starting to build your credit history, I would first request a credit line increase and then add one line every 6 months to be safe. I'd prioritize credit cards over charge cards, unless there was an offer that was too good to pass up. Remember, charge cards, won't deepen your credit line, so any expenses you put on them only contribute to your credit use and not your available credit. After you've established your credit for a couple of years, you could start to ramp this up. But until you have below 10 percent utilization and a couple of years of 100 percent on-time payment history, I would keep a modest pace.

- **Rebuilding Your Credit:** If you've found yourself with credit woes like I had in my early 20s, the more modest your approach to sign-ups the better. What I wanted to do was repair my credit score so I could easily get credit, whether it was for a home mortgage, an auto loan, or even an apartment lease. Luckily, I had a credit card with a history and could inquire about line increases as my score improved. If I was starting from scratch, or had my cards canceled, I'd have pursued a different approach via a secured card with the hope of converting it to an unsecured card, and then requesting deeper lines of credit prior to adding more cards. If you're unfamiliar with a secured credit card, it works like this: You put $500 down on the card, then every purchase you make is deducted from the balance. You refill the card as needed to make more purchases, rinse and repeat. Every 6 months I would have inquired about either converting my secured card to an unsecured card, then deepening my credit line, or getting an additional card with the same bank.

- **Established Credit:** If you have an established credit history and are looking to strategically add cards for their benefits, welcome offers, and travel hacking, I'd suggest no more than one new card every few months. This is general advice and doesn't take into account the nuances of bank rules, but from a broad credit health perspective, I have followed this strategy and incurred little to no credit health implications.

- **Applying for a Home Loan:** If you're looking to buy a home, I would avoid any and all sign-ups for 6 months. Recent inquiries and new lines of credit carry more weight in this specific situation, and you'll help yourself out in the long run by just hitting pause for a while.

5. Types of Credit or Credit Mix (10 percent)

Credit cards, auto leases, home loans, personal loans, utilities, apartment leases that report, and basically anything that requires you to make an installment payment on an asset or where a service is leased to you are all types of credit and diversify your credit mix. Your credit mix accounts for a very small portion of your credit score (10 percent), and, honestly, I've had a lot of different kinds of credit extended to me but have rarely seen much change to my score.

If you're at the beginning of your credit journey, it could be advantageous to be a cosigner on various kinds of credit. Let's say, for instance, you're in college and your parents have agreed to pay for part of a car or apartment lease. While they could do it in their name, what would be most advantageous to you is for you to be on it as well, with them as guarantors or co-lessees. This would establish another line of credit for you plus give you credit history.

"Zach, is there any way to get rent to show up on my credit report?"

Some leasing companies do this, however, in my experience most smaller companies do not. So it's definitely possible that your rent is being reported and you may not realize it. This is another good reason to always get your annual credit report.

I'm currently working with a business called Bilt, a fintech (financial technology) company shaking up the rental market by allowing people to pay their rent with their credit card with no fee. One of the services they provide is credit reporting. Renters in their alliance can seamlessly pay their rent via their app, but if your apartment isn't a part of the alliance, you can still pay through their app and they will mail your landlord a check. Rent is one of the biggest expenses many people have, and this is an incredible benefit to responsible renters who otherwise wouldn't have all those on-time payments reflected on their credit report.

"Zach, I only have one or two types of credit. Should I be concerned?"

Not at all. You can certainly have top-tier credit with a single type of credit. The biggest things to focus on are paying in full, on time, and working that utilization rate down to a single digit. If you're doing that, you're good to go!

FAQS

Is it bad to close credit cards?

The act of closing a credit card has a minimal effect on your credit score. What actually hurts it most is losing the line of credit. This is why I advocate for requesting a downgrade on any credit card that has an annual fee to one that doesn't have that annual fee. When you downgrade a card, that line of credit stays open even though the credit card product may change, which means the average age and history of that account continues to live on. When I say "product" I mean the specific branding of the card (e.g., a Chase Sapphire Preferred downgraded to a Chase Freedom Flex). It's the best of all worlds.

Still want to close it? You can request that your credit line be rotated onto another card that you have with the bank. Often, banks will allow you to combine lines of credit when you don't want to keep a card but do want to keep the line of credit associated with it. This works in reverse as well if you've been rejected for a credit card because the bank has given you all the credit it can give you. You can often request that a credit line be moved from an existing line and reallocated to the new card. This would allow you to take advantage of possible credit card sign-up bonuses.

Should I keep a small balance on my card?

Absolutely not. The goal is to pay zero interest and pay your bills in full and on time. I have seen this question on social media a lot, along with some horrendous advice that says carrying a balance will help your credit score. Carrying a balance not only adds to your utilization rate, but it also erodes your purchasing power and savings through high interest rates.

Remember that utilization is reported every month when your statement closes. If you pay the balance off in full, it still shows that you're using the credit allotted to you.

How can I get a perfect credit score?

There isn't really any concrete method for doing this, and you may lose out on a lot of fantastic credit card sign-up bonuses trying to chase a number that doesn't do anything other than give you bragging rights. I would instead advocate that your goal be to maintain a credit score that yields the lowest interest rate when it comes time to borrow for a large purchase like a home or automobile. I pursue a number in the high 700s to low 800s. This gives me enough cushion to add on lines of credit without the concern that the temporary hit to my credit will drop me below the 740 to 760 threshold that defines the top tier.

Should my significant other get their own card or be an authorized user on mine?

Can I say both? Each person would benefit from having their own separate line of credit. They can even be linked to the same bank account. But having different cards means more welcome offers, better credit for each person, and ultimately the ability to earn a lot more benefits and points. Two big advantages of having someone as an authorized user are the extension of specific card benefits to each cardholder and the ability to move points into programs in the authorized user's name. I'll explain this in more detail later.

How do you keep your credit score healthy, Zach?

I open and close new accounts all the time, and it seems like this should have a negative effect on my credit score since I'm losing accounts and potentially lines of credit and decreasing the average age of my credit by doing this. While this is true in theory, as you've learned, you can use the system to facilitate chasing the best deals for your wallet *and* keep your score high. I open five to ten cards per year and focus on strategy.

- Always, always, always pay on time and in full. This is the bedrock of your credit, and if you miss payments or fail to pay, it'll be a long road to recovery.

- Never cancel a card within 12 months of opening it. Worst case, you cancel around 380 days after opening it, but it's something I try to avoid altogether.

- Downgrade, don't cancel a card if possible. If you're carrying a card with an annual fee, downgrade it to one that has no annual fee, or at least a much cheaper one. Downgrading keeps the line of credit open. This keeps your utilization rate lower, since you have the credit available to you but use very little of it. Keeping the credit line open also adds to your average age of credit.

- Always keep your oldest card open. This will help your average age of credit.

- If you must cancel a card, rotate your credit. Often (not always) if you are canceling a card, you can rotate the credit onto another card you have with the bank. This means you can keep a similar depth of credit even though you're losing the line itself.

- Prioritize business cards over personal cards. If you have a small business, prioritize cards for it over those for your personal use. Most of those cards don't report monthly spending, which helps keep your utilization rate low.

RECAP

Now you have all the building blocks to start constructing your wallet. You understand the difference between your credit report and credit score, why you should pay the most attention to your FICO score, and which factors will ultimately move the needle most in maintaining and improving your FICO score.

Next, let's crack open your wallet, take a peek inside, and make sure you're carrying the cards that align best with your goals!

YOUR WALLET NEEDS TO SERVE YOUR GOALS

You work hard for your money, and when you spend it, it should be working hard for you. Most people don't put their wallets to work for them. All those swipes, inserts, and taps aren't aligned with what they really want. Personally, my goal is to travel the world as often and as luxuriously as possible. I'm willing to put in a lot of effort to keep track of everything because the return on that investment is massive to me. My goal is very different from someone who just wants the most cash back on their purchases with the least amount of effort. Neither person is right or wrong, but we need very different wallets. Your wallet needs to serve your goals, and in order to build that wallet, you need to understand the tools that are available.

The credit card marketplace has grown into an absolute jungle. There are airline cards, hotel cards, bank cards, cash-back cards, department store cards, virtual cards, the list goes on and on. It's easy to get lost and confused, and most people do. The marketplace is bound to get even more complicated as digital assets are adopted and the entire decentralized finance (DeFi) ecosystem evolves with its credit product offerings as well.

So how do you know which cards to add, cancel, and keep in your wallet? There isn't any fixed answer to that question. The cards you keep are a result of a strategy you're employing to get the results you desire. Your strategy can be as simple or complicated as you want, but the cards are a result of it, not the other way around. The further you go down the rabbit hole of travel hacking, the more skilled you will become, and the easier it will be for you to pursue your strategy.

When I realized the level of travel that points made available to me, it was clear what my goals were: fly insane first-class and business-class cabins as often as possible.

If there is anything that is unequivocal, it's this: Once you fly flat, you never wanna go back.

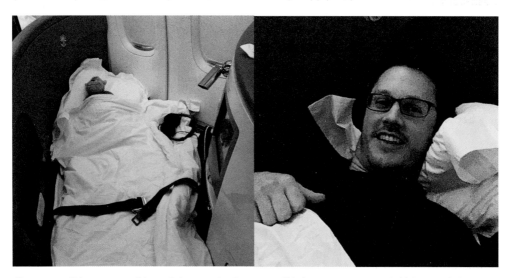

Can you tell how excited I was? It was the first time I'd done a review with Miles, and the crew absolutely loved him. The picture on the left is what happened when I popped into the bathroom to change into my pajamas (a rare amenity that Virgin Atlantic provides to its upper class passengers). I thought perhaps I'd get a lot of strange looks—a grown man carrying a stuffed animal around—but most people are along for the fun.

I'm not bothered by flying economy class on a two-hour flight from Atlanta to Detroit; give me an aisle seat, and I'm good to go. But after my first time flying flat to London (it was on a Virgin Atlantic flight from San Francisco to London's Heathrow Airport in the nose of a 747 that I got for 62,500 Delta SkyMiles and $5.60—it would have cost over $5,000 cash, just in case you were wondering), I knew I never wanted to go back to long-haul economy. Ever. I mean, they give you free champers and slippers! I knew I had to figure out how to do that over and over again.

So then, what are your goals?

Are you looking to establish or repair your credit? Do you want to get a steady flow of cash back? Do you have a few cards that you put most of your expenses on, and now you're looking to supplement those with a card that gives you free bag checks and priority boarding? Do you want to achieve a specific hotel status and need elite night credits to do so? Are you looking to take a really dope trip every few years? Or are you like me? Do you lust after the very best the world of travel has to offer, and you're willing to build a legion of credit cards only a three-ring binder will hold to make it happen?

There isn't a right or wrong answer, but each of these goals leads to a different strategy and each strategy employs one of three different kinds of credit cards:

Cash-back cards

- Earn cash back on your expenses.

Fixed-currency cards

- Earn bank points, airlines miles, or hotel points.

Flexible-currency cards

- Earn bank points that can be converted into other loyalty program currencies.

"Zach, I have no idea where to even begin."

Trust me, you're in great company. Most people I talk to don't know the difference between an American Express Gold card and an American Express Delta SkyMiles Gold card and why they'd choose one over the other. Let's break down each category of credit card so you understand the differences, and then you can make the most informed decision as to where you want to start, and how you want to build.

CASH-BACK CREDIT CARDS

At face value, these are the most straightforward cards on the market. You know what you spend and what the cash-back rate associated with your credit card is, so you can rest easy knowing you're getting a little something back. Some cards offer different rates of cash back depending on the category—gas, groceries, mobile phone bill, in-store purchases (think Costco)—but on every statement it's very easy to calculate exactly how much money you've received in cash back.

I would also add digital asset/cryptocurrency credit cards to this category, simply because most of them are giving a yield in bitcoin or some other cryptocurrency. I'm not going to unpack the nuances of cryptocurrency here, but the underlying principle is the same. You spend a certain amount and receive a cash-back yield on your purchases.

Cash-back cards have a fixed rate of return that is easy to understand. That's the appeal. Cash-back cards generally offer the following:

Earn from 1 percent to 2 percent cash back on all purchases.
- Spend $1,000, get $10 to $20 back.

    Usually this is paid in the form of:
    - » A statement credit.
    - » The ability to redeem it for certain items within a bank's portal.
    - » A deposit right into your bank account, or in a check.

Certain categories of purchases earn more cash back.
- Gas, groceries, streaming, dining, etc.

Cash back can be merged with flexible points.
- Some banks allow you to merge your cash back with their flexible points currencies, enhancing the value in excess of the cash back.

Cash-back cards can often be the very best choice for a lot of people. I'd even argue that if you're able to effectively earn a rate over $0.02 back per dollar you spend, you'll be beating most people with airline or hotel cards.

Why?

Most people don't get a lot of value out of their airline or hotel credit cards because they don't really know why they're using them. They think they're maximizing the system, but the system is actually maximizing them. Sure, you could argue that inflation erodes the value of cash, but airline and hotel programs notoriously devalue their programs in the dead of night and without warning. Most airlines used to publish award charts, so you'd have an idea of what your points are worth. Very few do this anymore.

Check your Delta, United, or American Airlines credit card and see what your points are generally worth. Unless you're being exceptionally strategic and flexible on when you can fly and where you're flying to, the odds are the number of miles you'll need to fly to your destination of choice, on the flight you want, will yield you much less than $0.02 a mile.

Let's take someone who spends roughly $2,500 a month, or $30,000 a year, on their card. If they used no-annual-fee cards that gave an average 2 percent cash back on purchases, they'd get $600 back in a year. Clear-cut. Straightforward. They can spend that money on whatever they want.

Now consider that same $30,000 per year being spent on a Delta card.

Currently the only no-fee Delta card earns 1 mile per dollar spent, or 1X, everywhere, 2X on dining, and 2X on Delta flights. Let's say somehow the cardholder was able to reach 1.5X miles per dollar spent on average. They would net 45,000 Delta SkyMiles ($30,000 at 1.5 miles per dollar). The biggest restriction is that these miles must be used within the Delta program.

In April of 2022, I needed to fly from Atlanta to New Orleans for the Freddie Awards. Here's an example of how Delta was pricing at the time I wanted to book my ticket.

Wed, Apr 20, 2022

Price includes taxes and fees. Baggage fee may apply. Services and amenities may vary or change.

	Main	Comfort+	First

Flight	Main	Comfort+	First
LOWEST FARE NEW WI-FI DL1418 1h 31m 7:20am ✈ 7:51am ATL Nonstop MSY Details | Seats	Main (L) **$171** One Way 4 left at this price	Sold Out	First (I) **$321** One Way 2 left at this price
NEW WI-FI DL2782 1h 36m 9:50am ✈ 10:26am ATL Nonstop MSY Details | Seats	Main (Q) **$269** One Way	Sold Out	First (C) **$619** One Way
NEW WI-FI DL2055 1h 28m 12:21pm ✈ 12:49pm ATL Nonstop MSY Details | Seats	Main (K) **$239** One Way	Sold Out	Sold Out

Wed, Apr 20, 2022

Price includes taxes and fees. Baggage fee may apply. Services and amenities may vary or change.

	Main	Comfort+	First

Flight	Main	Comfort+	First
LOWEST FARE NEW WI-FI DL1418 1h 31m 7:20am ✈ 7:51am ATL Nonstop MSY Details | Seats	Main (N) **14,500** + $6 One Way 4 left at this price	Sold Out	First (O) **42,000** + $6 One Way 5 left at this price
NEW WI-FI DL2782 1h 36m 9:50am ✈ 10:26am ATL Nonstop MSY Details | Seats	Main (N) **23,500** + $6 One Way	Sold Out	First (O) **56,000** + $6 One Way
NEW WI-FI DL2055 1h 28m 12:21pm ✈ 12:49pm ATL Nonstop MSY Details | Seats	Main (N) **20,500** + $6 One Way	Sold Out	Sold Out

With 45,000 SkyMiles to use, what the cardholder would like to see is a rate of return in excess of $600, since they must use them within this program and are not free to use them anywhere, like they would be with cash back. What can be seen here is redemptions ranging between 0.75 cent per point (the 7:20 a.m. flight that is 42,000 miles or $321 in first class) and just under 1.2 cents on the economy redemptions.

- At 0.75 cent a point, they'd get $337.50 of Delta flights for 45,000 points.
- At 1.2 cents a point, they'd get $540.

This is cherry picking to a point. But I'd argue that not only is this par for the course, it underlines why I contend that a lot of people may be better off using cash-back cards if they don't use any other credit card benefits, have no ambition to take aspirational trips, and just want to sit back and rest easy.

"But Zach, you don't typically use cash-back cards, right?"

Yes and no. I have quite a few cash-back cards that, if they lived alone in my wallet, they would earn cash back. However, when they are paired with premium credit cards in the same family, the banks that issue them allow me to merge the points and supercharge them into points that can be transferred into other programs. So if I want to use them for cash back, I can, but if I want to combine them to transfer into partner programs, I can do that too.

Good examples of this are the Citi Double Cash and Citi Premier cards. Both of these cards earn Citi ThankYou Rewards points. The Citi Premier earns premium ThankYou points that can be transferred into over a dozen transfer partners. The Citi Double Cash earns 2 percent cash back (which they called ThankYou points) that can be redeemed toward a statement credit or on specific items in the Citi ThankYou portal, but they can't be transferred to partners. Unless . . .

If you carry a Citi Double Cash alongside the Citi Premier, you can combine all of the points you earn from your Citi Double Cash with those from your Citi Premier account. Once combined, they can be transferred into any of over a dozen partner programs where you may get substantially higher redemption values.

You may be wondering, why not just carry the Citi Premier?

(Disclaimer, I didn't dislocate my arm to get this selfie, although the angle is everything, am I right?)

As I mentioned, most cash-back cards don't have an annual fee, but they often have an increased rate of return on everyday spending.

- Citi Double Cash earns 2 percent back on all purchases with no bonus categories.

- Citi Premier earns 3X on travel, gas, groceries, and dining, but 1X everywhere else.

Having both cards in my wallet means I'll earn no less than 2X on all my purchases with some great 3X category bonuses, and it doesn't cost me anything to keep the cash-back card. I've used Citi ThankYou points to book a $5,000-plus first-class ticket from Germany to the US for 87,000 Avianca LifeMiles by transferring ThankYou Points to Avianca when they showed availability. That's a redemption value of over 5 cents a point, and I'm earning a minimum of 2X on all my purchases, meaning I'm effectively getting 10 cents back on every purchase I make.

Are you starting to see how you can use the system to your advantage?

"Zach, you also carry airline and hotel credit cards, right?"

Absolutely. In fact, these cards can have a lot of value, but you need to understand how you unlock that value. Airline and hotel credit cards are part of a category that I call fixed-currency credit cards. Let's unpack how they can best be used in your wallet.

FIXED-CURRENCY CREDIT CARDS

When I talk about the points and miles that programs create for their members, I refer to them in a colloquial sense as currency. I realize that this doesn't fit the exact definition of a currency, but for our purposes, it's how I use the term. (And I'm the author, so I'm going to give myself some leeway.) Fixed-currency credit cards earn you points or miles that can only be redeemed within the program that issues it. In other words, they can't be converted into the currency of another loyalty program the way "flexible currency" programs allow.

These cards could add good value to your wallet if you're using them for the right reasons, but they are part of your supporting cast of cards. They serve a purpose, but because they only earn points that are siloed in a program, I strongly advocate against putting all of your ordinary spending on them.

For instance, even if your overall goal is to get as much cash back as possible, having an airline credit card may save you a lot of money every other year on bag fees. Keeping a hotel card that earns a free annual night certificate could come in handy on a road trip. I could go on and on, but these cards could help you save a lot of money, well in excess of the card's annual fee, when you do decide to take a trip. Even if travel isn't your primary objective with your wallet, they can be quite valuable when used effectively.

There are four general categories of fixed-currency credit cards:

- Department store credit cards, which may earn cash back or points redeemable for store purchases
- Bank points, which must be used in the bank's portal or redemption options stipulated by the bank program, but not transferred out into partner programs
- Airline credit cards, which must be used on the airline program the credit card is associated with
- Hotel credit cards, which must be used within the hotel program the credit card is associated with

Department Store Credit Cards
Let's start with one you've been offered a million times.

"Would you like to open a J.Crew, Saks Fifth Avenue, Macy's, Nordstrom, Lowe's, or Home Depot credit card and save 20 percent on your purchase today?"

We've all been there. It's tempting, right? The savings is immediate, and if you're making a massive purchase, it could be worth it. But over the long term, the rewards are very limited, and I certainly believe there are far better options for your wallet. That doesn't mean they couldn't be used in your strategy. But I can tell you I don't have a single one. With that said, let's break down how they work and whether they could be useful to you.

Some department store credit cards can only be used in the store itself, and others allow you to use them anywhere. Generally speaking, "department store" credit cards offer the following incentive structure:

Earn cash back on purchases.

- Some cards offer cash back on purchases you make anywhere you use the card.
- Most offer cash back only at the store that issues it, for example, 5 percent off Lowe's purchases.

Earn points on purchases you make in store, or anywhere.

- These points are only redeemable at the store for goods and services.

My experience has been that you'll be lucky to redeem the points for a penny apiece. Meaning, you'd be better off using another credit card that earns points at a higher rate or a cash-back card that gets 2 cents or more on every purchase.

"Are there reasons I'd want to use a department store credit card, Zach?"

Great question ;). Let's say you're in the real estate business and spend a lot of money at Lowe's. If they're willing to give you up to 5 percent cash back on a lot of your purchases, and you're not earning store points but you're getting that back in the form of a statement credit, or just straight off the top, that's a really solid deal. As an example, if you're a contractor spending $1 million a year at Lowe's, it could be very advantageous. If Lowe's gives you an average of 3 to 4 percent savings on your $1 million spend, you're saving $30,000 to 40,000. You'd be hard pressed to outdo that kind of ROI (return on investment) with any other form of credit card with the flexibility of cash.

"How could I get a comparable rate with a flexible currency card?"

There are two possible options: gift cards and shopping portals.

Certain credit cards give bonuses at grocery stores or office supply stores. You could go to those stores and buy gift cards for the department store of your choice. For instance, if you wanted to make a $5,000 purchase at Lowe's, you could use your Chase Ink Business Cash which earns 5X points at office supply stores. You may even be able to make that purchase online, get virtual gift cards, and then purchase $5,000 worth of stuff at Lowe's earning 5X Chase points.

One way you could tap higher rates of return would be to access Lowe's via a shopping portal (which we will speak about in more detail later). The big downside here is that you would need to order everything online rather than make purchases in the store, and sometimes you can't stack the discounts.

Are you thinking what I'm thinking? Yes, you may be able to use your Chase Ink Business Cash card earning 5X points to buy Lowe's gift cards, then use those gift cards in a portal earning even more points per dollar.

"Zach, I've seen department store credit cards that earn good rates of cash back."

I would consider these to be cash-back cards in department store clothing. Currently, a good example of this would be the Costco credit card. They lure you to Costco by offering up to 4 percent cash back when you use it at gas stations, 2 percent in store, but also a decent return elsewhere. If you do a lot of spending at Costco, this could be advantageous, and not a terrible use elsewhere. However, this isn't the case for most department store branded credit cards. Most of them lure you in with an instant discount at checkout and then give you points that have very little flexibility and must be spent in store at suboptimal levels.

"Would a department store card help my credit score?"

Yep, as I mentioned earlier, if the card issues you a line of credit, it would add to your overall amount of credit available, which could help lower your usage number.

"Should I cancel my department store credit card?"

This totally depends on how much accounting you want to do. If you remember to use it at the store, continue to extract value from it, and it doesn't have an annual fee, keep it. It could also add to your average age of credit and deepen your credit line, both of which would be beneficial. Additionally, it wouldn't hurt you if it lived in a sock drawer and you never used it, and only kept it for the reasons I mentioned above.

"Why wouldn't I want to use a department store credit card?"

The biggest reason is the complexity it adds to your wallet. In certain situations, it can make sense, especially if you're making a lot of purchases at a specific store. But if you're only occasionally frequenting that store, it doesn't make sense, and you may be able to earn an increased rate of return using shopping portals or buying gift cards. This aligns more with my goal of earning points I can use to take business-class and first-class flights to faraway places.

Miles enjoying American Airlines business class to Japan

I have an entire section dedicated to shopping portals starting on page 100. These are an incredibly effective way to earn a lot of extra cash back, or your favorite points, at the stores you frequent most with very little friction involved.

For instance, if you needed a few thousand American Airlines miles in order to book a business-class ticket, and you had a large purchase at Lowe's, you could leverage that purchase to earn the needed miles by using the American Airlines shopping portal. Every dollar you spend in the portal earns American miles.

Let's say American Airlines shopping portal was offering 5X at Lowe's if you made your purchase in the shopping portal. You'd start your order in their portal, it would populate the Lowe's website, and you could make your purchase as you normally would. The difference is the portal coding would earn you an extra 5X American Airlines miles instead of just loading the website directly. Pretty neat, right?

If you used an Amex card that earns 2X everywhere to make the purchase, you'd earn those 2X Amex points plus 5X via the American Airlines portal, so 7X in total. Your credit card could be earning Amex points while the portal is earning you American Airlines miles, so you're blending your earning as well. You could even add in your Lowe's loyalty number and earn their points too. To make the math easy, we will assign a value of 1.5 cents to each of those points, meaning that the 7X points you could earn via the portal would yield a 10.5 percent return on your purchase.

It could be worth a lot more than that if those points were pushing you over the threshold to fly like this. I surprised my wife for her 30th birthday with a trip to Japan for the weekend. We enjoyed American Airlines business class on the way over.

There are certainly arguments for having a department store credit card. For some people, it can be worthwhile, but for most, it's another card to juggle that doesn't add a lot of value to your wallet unless you're a hard-core shopper at a specific store. Even then, there are ways to earn the same number of points, or even more, without adding additional cards to your wallet.

Fixed-Currency Bank Points

Fixed-currency bank points can only be redeemed for a fixed rate in a bank's portal. You may earn multiple points per dollar on these cards, or a single point per dollar, but when it comes time for redemption, the value is fixed. There isn't any way for you to redeem your points for a value higher than the bank dictates.

Effectively, I don't really see a point in keeping these cards in your wallet outside of maybe getting one for a large sign-up bonus and then dumping it after a year.

Going back to our example of spending $2,500 a month, $30,000 in a year, and earning 1.5X on that spend, you'd end up with 45,000 points. If your card allows you to redeem those points for a penny apiece, you have $450 in value, but it's limited to the portal and items the bank allows you to redeem them on. Some portals will give you 1.5X cents in travel redemption, or $675 in this example. Effectively, you're buying tickets within the travel portal by redeeming your points to purchase that travel.

The bank's travel portal is powered by a consolidator or travel search engine of some sort, and you're captive to how it prices your travel. Oftentimes other consolidators, the airline, or the hotel itself will price things more competitively, plus you may be able to earn more points via other booking portals rather than the bank's. At the end of the day, I think there is a pretty solid argument that it's not worth keeping a fixed-currency bank card as your primary card rather than a flexible currency card or even a cash-back card.

I'll get into flexible currency cards in more detail, but there are versions of them that not only allow you to redeem within a travel portal, but they also let you transfer them to partners where redemption values can go through the roof. Be still my travel hacking heart!

"Despite your excellent advice, are there any reasons why I'd still get a fixed-currency bank card?"

There are a couple of notable exceptions. One could be that the credit card offers up some really great benefits as a cardholder that outweigh the annual fee. The second would be when you can earn a large sign-up bonus. For example, let's say you could earn a 100,000-point bonus after spending $4,000 in 3 months. Well, you've earned yourself $1,000 to $1,500 worth of travel on just a $4,000 spend. Pretty sweet deal, even if the bank's travel portal prices your trip a little higher than other places.

There are always exceptions, but making a fixed-currency bank card the focus of your wallet isn't what I'd recommend. I'd only use fixed-currency cards as supporting characters. Not the main role. The same goes for airline and hotel credit cards.

Airline and Hotel Credit Cards
It's all about the bennies, baybay!

Simply put. The main reason you want to keep airline and hotel credit cards is for the benefits they provide, not the points they earn. This is where people go wrong: It's not keeping these cards in your wallet that is misaligning your strategy, but how you end up using them that misses the mark. Airline and hotel cards can be wonderful supporting characters if you know how they are best used. So let's get into their best uses.

Generally speaking, airline and hotel credit cards offer some of the following benefits:

- Free checked bags
- A buy-one-get-one ticket deal
- A free night every year, up to a certain category or number of points
- Elite miles or a spending waiver

- Cardholder discounts or promotions
- Preferred boarding and check-in
- Hotel elite status
- Spend your way to top-tier elite status
- Lounge access

Each of these benefits has a value associated with it, and everyone is going to assess these differently. If you know you're planning a couple of big family trips and waived bag fees for a family of five would save you hundreds of dollars, that's a great reason to pick up a card associated with the airline you'll be traveling. You may even get priority boarding and check-in as well. You don't need to put all your expenses on that card throughout the year to enjoy those benefits. In fact, as long as you pay the annual fee, the benefits are usually available.

Another great reason for keeping an airline credit card as a supporting player is if you're a regular traveler who enjoys lounge access. Delta and American Airlines have both offered a premium credit card that includes SkyClub or Admirals Club access, respectively, as a cardholder perk. Here's the crazy part. The annual fee on the card is less than what the airline charges for access, and oftentimes you can add on authorized users who get their own access as well! These premium cards usually come with a baggage perk, priority boarding, priority check-in, etc. If you and your family fly Delta or American a ton, and value having guaranteed lounge access, it could be extremely worthwhile to you and make a lot of sense to keep it in your wallet. It doesn't mean you want to put all your spending on the card though.

Hotel credit cards work in a very similar way. They are fantastic supporting characters.

Elizabeth and I keep a few hotel credit cards purely for the benefits associated with them. For instance, I have an old IHG Hotels & Resorts credit card that I pay $49 a year for, and it comes with two benefits that make it a complete no-brainer. The first benefit is a free night issued on our cardholder anniversary. In fact, I'd say we typically redeem our free night for at least $200, but often well over $300 when we use it in big cities. I view it as a win as long as I redeem my free night for more than $49 a year. But that's not all. The card also comes with a perk that gives us 10 percent back on all the points we use in a year up to 100,000 points. My family has saved 100,000 points several times over the years just because of the rebate—yes, my mom, dad, and I all have one.

(Free the nipple, I say.)

Several years ago, IHG and Chase announced they were going to introduce a new card. We feared they would eliminate the benefits of our old card or force us into getting the new version. Nope. They allowed the grandfathering of the old card and its benefits to continue onward. Byah! (That's what I say when I'm happy. It's a long story, but try it. It feels good to exclaim it. *Byah!*)

When details of that new IHG card were revealed, I couldn't believe my eyes. They included an anniversary night again plus members would get a 4th night free on all award stays. The best part? If you had the old card, you could combine the benefits of both of these cards on a single stay. Obviously I applied, and the greatest single stay value came during my honeymoon.

We stayed 5 nights at Six Senses Maldives in an overwater villa and used points to book the entire thing. Give it a Google; the resort is insane and regularly charges over $1,000 per night for our overwater villa. This is what points and miles are all about: experiencing aspirational bucket list items that ordinarily you'd never pay the money to do.

What did we do? Points obvs. And with a monster discount at that!

Ordinarily, the hotel charges 100,000 points per night, which would have set us back 500,000 points. That's a serious haul of points. But because we had these two IHG credit cards, we received a 4th night free, knocking the cost down to 400,000 points, and then we received 10 percent back, or 40,000 points, totaling 360,000 points. The best part? IHG was selling those points earlier in the year for 0.4 cents apiece, meaning instead of paying over $5,000 like most people staying on the island, our technique meant we could have paid just $1,800, or about $360 a night. (We kept that news to ourselves at the all-inclusive breakfasts.)

Here's a look at the view from the free breakfast we enjoyed, as a result of our status we got through the credit card, at the Waldorf Astoria in Dubai.

"Do all hotel credit cards come with a free night?"

Typically, hotel credit cards that have an annual fee issue a free night after your cardholder anniversary. There are exceptions, and of course there are some limitations, but ordinarily just that free night alone is worth far more than the annual fee.

"Do any credit cards give hotel elite status?"

- Some cards give you straight up elite status just for being a cardholder.
  » Amex Platinum, which is a flexible currency card, has long given Marriott and Hilton elite status.
- Other cards will give you elite nights that help you get closer to status.

The Amex Hilton Aspire Card gives us top-tier elite status with Hilton. We get hotel club access, free breakfasts, and suite upgrades, so it makes a lot of sense for us to pay the $450 annual fee because we extract a lot of value.

A massive one bedroom suite at the Conrad New York Midtown just a couple blocks south of Central Park

Rarely, unless we're staying at a property associated with that credit card or there is a great promotion, do we ever use those airline or hotel credit cards for our everyday expenses. Instead, we pay the annual fees, extract the benefits, and use different cards for everyday purchases that are more rewarding and yield a much higher return.

My wife and I recently redeemed a free night certificate from a Hilton-branded credit card at the Conrad New York Midtown in New York City. Before we even checked in, we were notified via the app that we had been upgraded to a one-bedroom suite, which regularly retails for $1,000 a night. That upgrade was undoubtedly a result of the top-tier status that came along with our credit card. Not only did we get a free night, we also got an incredible upgrade.

"OK Zach, I understand that the benefits are worthwhile, but why not earn the points or miles on them as well?"

Simply because your points are stuck in that program's silo of redemption.

If you have a Delta credit card, and all your spending goes on it, you'll only have Delta miles when it comes time to take a trip. You can still use the benefits of the card without putting your expenses on it, but if you do, those miles can only be redeemed at the price Delta dictates, and on Delta or its partners. What happens if Delta doesn't have access to award space to London, but American Airlines does? Or before you have a chance to use your hard-earned miles, Delta changes all of their award pricing? You won't have other options because all of your awards are tied up in a single program. All your eggs are in one basket if you will (which, just so you know, is a touchy subject for me because I'm on an elimination diet and eggs are not allowed). You want options because award space and programs are always changing, and, unlike my gut, you need to be fluid.

The good news is (drumroll) you can have it both ways! Most airline and hotel programs are transfer partners of flexible currency programs, meaning you can trade bank points in for the airline and hotel points you need for a specific booking.

FLEXIBLE-CURRENCY CREDIT CARDS

Flexible points are the crème de la crème on the points and miles menu. Not only can you redeem them for whatever your bank offers you in their portal, but you have the flexibility to turn them into airline or hotel points via a transfer partner. And these transfer partners . . . oh, you'd better sit down . . . these bad boys are the key to traveling like your bank account balance has a couple of extra zeroes at the end of it. Love this tone!

Flexible points have these important attributes:

- They can be used within the bank's portal for redemptions.
  - » Travel, products, services, sometimes even statement credits.
- They can be transferred into partner programs.
  - » Turn your bank points into partner program points.

The best flexible points transfer in a 1:1 ratio to most of their partners:

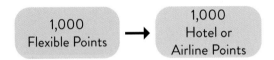

Credit cards that earn flexible points are the main characters of your wallet. As the main character, you want to streamline your expenses onto these cards and then build your supporting cast of cards around them to add benefits and additional value. The idea behind the strategy is to give you the most options when it comes time to use them for travel. There is no such thing as a store of value when it comes to points, but flexible point accounts are the closest thing. Why? Until you're ready to book a trip, you don't know what program you'll ultimately want to use to book it, because you won't know who has the award availability, the best routing, fewest surcharges, etc. By storing your points in an account that has access to a variety of redemption options, including transfer programs, you're doing your best to ensure that when it comes time to use them, you'll be able to unlock their greatest potential.

Currently the following programs earn flexible currency points:

- American Express Membership Rewards
- Bilt Rewards
- Brex
- Capital One Miles
- Chase Ultimate Rewards
- Citi ThankYou Rewards
- Marriott Bonvoy Points

Now just because your card is associated with one of these programs doesn't mean it has flexible points. Each of these programs have their own ecosystem full of credit card products that have different annual fees, included benefits, category bonus rates, and even different redemption values based on the cards you keep. These ecosystems are constantly changing, new products are being introduced, old ones are being overhauled, and it's easy to get lost in the weeds. It really comes down to this.

Do your main characters:

- Earn bonus points on categories where you spend the most?
- Earn points that transfer to airlines that are a part of the big three airline alliances?
- Earn points that can access hotel programs?
- Have access to at least two of the programs above that share some partners, but also have some that are unique to each program?

If the core cast of your wallet is two or three cards that fulfill those requirements, you are good to go. From there you'd add or subtract airline or hotel credit cards that add value via their benefits. At the end of each year, you'd have a quick look to make sure you're extracting more value than the annual fee, and voilà, you're well on your way to becoming a travel hacker.

"What do you mean by 'earn bonus points on categories where I spend the most'?"

Every purchase you make is coded by the bank who processes the payment. These codes put your purchases into categories that the bank may incentivize with category bonuses. This is a way you can really earn a lot of points where you spend the most.

Some of the most common categories are:

- Supermarkets
- Gas stations
- Travel
- Office supply stores
- Pharmacies

- Streaming services
- Dining
- Rideshares
- Online ad spending
- Airfare
- The list goes on

If you have a long-distance relationship and spend loads on flights and gas to see each other, you want to make sure you have a card that earns you bonus points on airline tickets and gas purchases. If you have a large family and are spending a ton on supermarkets and restaurants, you'd want a card that gives you bonus points on groceries and dining. If you have a leaky gut and sometimes have to rush home from a dinner, and your wife has the car keys, so you order an Uber because otherwise . . . well, you get it. Wherever you spend the most, you want to make sure you're getting multiple points per dollar and then supplement that card with another one that earns 1.5X to 2X on all purchases regardless of category.

For instance, you may carry an Amex Gold because it offers 4X on US supermarkets and dining, but also a Capital One Venture X since it gives 2X everywhere. Both cards earn flexible points and have some crossover partners.

"What do you mean 'have access to the big three airline alliances'?"

The vast majority of the airlines in the world belong to one of the following three airline alliances:

- Star Alliance
- SkyTeam
- oneworld

Cue the Game of Thrones *theme song, Miles and I are enjoying our "Throne" seat on Swiss Air business class.*

You want to be earning as many points as possible that give you access to all three of the major airline alliances. Why? The super cool thing about these alliances is that the member airlines of each alliance have access to some of the award space of their partner airlines, and oftentimes, the lounges, early boarding, baggage, check-in, and other benefits that each airline's elite members have.

Why is this cool?

Let's say you have a bunch of Chase Ultimate Rewards and want to go to Europe. One cool way to fly business class to Europe is on Swiss Air, specifically in what they call "the throne" seat.

How do you use your Chase Ultimate Rewards to book it?

Well, first of all, Chase Ultimate Rewards are flexible and can be used to book Swiss business class in a couple of different ways. First, you could redeem your points in their travel portal at a rate that is based on the card you hold. For instance, Chase Sapphire Preferred gives you 1.25 cents for every Ultimate Rewards you have toward a travel redemption. But have you seen business-class prices? A one-way ticket may cost you $5,000. That would cost you a whopping 400,000 Ultimate Rewards. The second way would be to make use of their transfer partners. Here are all of the travel partners of Chase Ultimate Rewards that you could convert Chase points into via transfer.

Chase Ultimate Rewards are fantastic flexible points.

Take a good look at the Chase Ultimate Rewards transfer partners, do you see Swiss anywhere? No, right? So then how do you go about booking that Swiss throne?

Cue: Star Alliance

Chase Ultimate Rewards can be transferred into United, Air Canada Aeroplan, or Singapore Airlines, which are all member airlines of Star Alliance. Airlines will release award space to their own members, but they'll also release award space to partners. If Swiss releases award space to its partners, you may end up having access to it. This is exactly how I booked the Swiss throne for a trip to Europe a few years ago. Let's use Air Canada's Aeroplan as an example.

If Swiss released award seats that were available to its partners, you could take 70,000 Ultimate Rewards, transfer them to Air Canada Aeroplan to book your Swiss business-class throne.

The biggest factor is making sure that you always look for award space before you transfer miles into a partner program. In this case, make sure that Aeroplan has award space available. Many times, I've noticed that United has access to a partner flight, but Singapore Airlines doesn't. Transfers are one way, and every partner doesn't have access to the same award space even if they are in an alliance together.

"Do airlines partner outside of an alliance?"

Absolutely, and the same strategy applies. For instance, Emirates and JetBlue are partners. JetBlue recently started flying from the East Coast of the US to London. When the cabins aren't full, they will release award space, and it's possible that Emirates could have access to it. If we had the same 70,000 Chase Ultimate Rewards as we had in the example before, we could either transfer to Emirates, or we could transfer to JetBlue. Look at the difference.

Here is the price to fly JetBlue Mint from New York to London if you were to use JetBlue points.

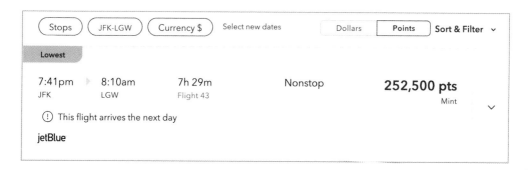

Now look what happens if we were to use Emirates points to book the same exact flight.

Pretty crazy, right? You could fly four times on JetBlue Mint between New York and London if you booked using Emirates miles for the same price that JetBlue charges using its own miles. Now Emirates won't always have access to that award space, but you can see the massive advantage in having the ability to book via Emirates rather than JetBlue.

Ultimately, you want to employ a strategy that affords you the ability to access as many programs as possible so that you can take advantage of these sweet spots whenever they present themselves. This is the big advantage of holding a flexible point card rather than an airline or hotel point card. You can still populate airline miles and hotel points with a transfer, but you aren't locked into that one currency.

"Airlines seem to offer some great value. Why do I need access to hotel programs?"

Admittedly, hotel programs can have some of the worst redemptions out there. But there is always the exception to the rule, and having access to these programs is incredibly worthwhile. As a rule of thumb, you never want to settle for less than a 1.5 cents to 2 cents redemption. I try to earn at least 2X points on all of my purchases, and if you're able to extract 1.5 cents to 2 cents on all your redemptions, you're actually getting a 3 cents to 4 cents return on your spending, which is head and shoulders above cash back. It is often harder to extract this kind of value from hotel programs than from business-class and first-class flights, but there are loads of times I've transferred into hotel programs to grab outsized value.

One of the most memorable times was in Bali after my wife's TV show wrapped its final season. We ended up flying west around the world on points visiting Singapore, Bali, Dubai, and Paris. One of the coolest stops was the Alila Villas perched on the cliffs of Uluwatu in Bali. It was my first time visiting an Alila property, and it was absolutely stunning. The entry-level room will set you back $1,000 a night. It's a full one-bedroom villa, with collapsing doors that open onto its own pool and indoor and outdoor showers, and, as luck would have it, it is part of a Hyatt program.

We stayed for 4 nights, and instead of paying $1,000 a night, we used 30,000 Hyatt points. That's a very good 3.3 cents valuation per point. The best part? Not only could you transfer points from Chase Ultimate Rewards and now Bilt Rewards, but at the time you could buy them for 1.8 cents apiece. If I can use points to experience hotels of this caliber and still get a phenomenal valuation, I'm a very happy camper.

Werk while working, that's what I say.

This is a picture of us right after check-in enjoying a refreshing drink in the lobby while our room was being prepared. Can you tell I'm feeling level ten smug? (It's all in the eyes.)

Hotel credit cards often come with annual night certificates. As this book ages, the programs will change how they issue these certificates, but the strategy will remain the same. For instance, the Hyatt credit card has long come with a free night that's correlated to your credit card account anniversary. Most people don't want to just spend a single night at a property, so having the ability to populate points to fill in around your free night adds value to your free night, since you can make it a part of a longer stay.

My buddy Dave and I went to Vietnam back in 2016 and stayed at the Park Hyatt Saigon—at the time it was charging well over $400 a night. Waaaaaaay more than we were willing to pay, but it was on my hotel bucket list for Southeast Asia and an incredible use of a free night certificate. We wanted to stay multiple days, so we ended up using a free night certificate for the first night and Hyatt points for the other nights, which we populated from Chase Ultimate Rewards.

The Park Hyatt Saigon was only 15,000 points per night (it still is as of May 2022), and we extracted around 3 cents per point, but we were also able to stay at the same hotel for multiple nights. The best part is we were also able to upgrade the other nights to a suite as a result of Dave's Hyatt Diamond status. Stacking those bennies!

Lufthansa First Class offers one of the most incredible experiences: exiting the lounge and being whisked across the tarmac in a chauff- eured Porsche straight to your waiting 747-8i where you're escorted directly to your seat.

"Why do you need access to more than one of these programs?"

The idea or strategy I invoke is similar to consolidating all of your points into one airline or hotel credit card, but with flexible points. Each program has access to its own list of partners, some cross over, some don't. Also, flexible point programs add and remove partners and promote transfer bonuses, and any way I can add options to my wallet, I will. I either have, or have had, points in every single transferable currency. I never want to encounter a situation where there is a trip I want to book, and I don't have the points to make it happen. There are often opportunities to buy points, so you can shore up the difference. But frequently the price isn't right, there are limitations, or the program I want to use doesn't sell them.

I also love the fact that many of the programs have similar transfer partners; this means I don't have to drain one account just to access a partner. I can spread transfers across multiple currencies. Let's say I wanted to fly Emirates first class to Milan. Emirates is currently a transfer partner of every single flexible currency. If I had points in Amex, Chase, Bilt, and Capital One, I could spread those deductions out across all four flexible currencies and still have balances in each. The main reason you'd want to do this is so that, should a redemption come up that is only accessible via one flexible currency, you could access it.

When I was planning my mom's trip around the world in 2017, we were fortunate to start with a healthy number of points, but most of those weren't in flexible programs. Primarily we were sitting on a bunch of Marriott and IHG points, since my parents have owned timeshares associated with those brands for a long time and could opt for points instead of using the timeshare. This was a great way to offset a few hotel stays, but the flights were the hardest things to lock up and coordinate.

At the time, Chase, Citi, and Amex were the only programs that had flexible currencies. Capital One was still mainly cash back, Brex and Bilt didn't even exist, and Marriott hadn't acquired SPG yet. So along with getting specific airline credit cards, I also put together a plan to accumulate as many Chase, Amex, and Citi points as we could get before the trip.

We are on a plane! Can you even believe that is a plane? And all for points!

One of the goals I had was for us to fly all together in Singapore Suites and Lufthansa first class. These are still two of the most aspirational and luxurious ways to fly around the planet. Not only are they outstanding in the air, but, when you fly first class with either of these airlines, it includes incredible ground experiences as well. Both airlines have private terminals just for their first-class passengers, and Lufthansa will go so far as to drive you between connecting flights. You feel like James Bond at the beginning of the movie when everything's going great and his Brioni suit is sharp as his wit and still wrinkle free.

As I'm sure you can imagine, finding award availability can be a bit tricky. These are two very difficult cabins to book three people into, and you really have to stay on top of award space. We got lucky with Singapore Suites when they released two seats on our route months ahead of time. I immediately booked tickets for my parents, and I was able to put myself on a waitlist that opened up shortly thereafter. This is an anomaly, but we had the points in place to take advantage as soon as the space was released.

Even though I had started putting the trip together well over a year before our first leg, I was fine-tuning everything while on the trip. Our final destination was Grasse, France, located roughly 30 minutes outside Cannes and famous for its perfumes. It was on our list because Grasse is the home of Molinard, the maker of Habanita, the perfume my mom has worn for over 50 years. Visiting the factory where it was made had been on her bucket list for as long as I could remember.

My dad had been in charge of coordinating the tour at the factory. He hit an absolute home run and managed to secure a private tour where we learned about the history of the brand and the process of making the perfume. My mom was over the moon. I really wanted to carry that momentum through the rest of the trip and was dead set on the final flight to the states being epic. That meant I had Lufthansa first class firmly in my sights. But Lufthansa doesn't traditionally release award space until a couple of weeks prior to departure, which was when we would be on our around-the-world tour. On top of that, Lufthansa might not release two seats at once. So what do you do?

Months in advance, I decided to book worst-case-scenario flights. If, for some reason, Lufthansa didn't release two seats, my parents would have a great flight back to the US anyways. So I booked them tickets in business class on Austrian using 65,000 Singapore miles to ensure they could fly back in business class. In the planning process we'd signed up for a couple of Amex and Chase cards, both of which were, and still are, transfer partners of Singapore. Singapore, Austrian, and Lufthansa are all part of Star Alliance. Do you see where I'm going here?

My goal was to monitor the Lufthansa first class award space while we were on the trip, and if it opened up, I would rebook the Austrian flights on Lufthansa first class. Since all three airlines were in the same alliance, I could use the same miles I booked the Austrian flights with to book the Lufthansa flights, and just pay the difference in miles and a change fee. At the time, it took anywhere from 4 to 48 hours for Singapore miles to populate the account after an Amex, Chase, or Citi transfer. I knew if Lufthansa opened up award space, I could rebook, but I couldn't risk losing the seats to someone else during a transfer period. When you book with points, if you cancel, you will get those points back (you'll often have to pay a cancellation fee, though).

Well before we started on the trip, I used my parents' Chase and Amex points and added the miles needed for first class. Instead of transferring in the 130,000 needed for both business-class flights, I transferred in 160,000, which was the rate for first class from Europe to the US at the time. I removed 80,000 from Chase and 80,000 from Amex. I then used 130,000 of the 160,000 to book the Austrian flight in business class, leaving a balance of 30,000, which was enough to book the Lufthansa tickets should they become available.

I felt pretty confident I'd be able to swing this. But I also told my folks, while on the trip, that we might need to adjust our final date in the South of France, but it'd be worth it. This is another aspect of award travel. The more flexible you are, the better the odds will be that you'll be able to fly in the best cabins. As for myself, I didn't book anything. For whatever reason, this kind of stuff excites me rather than stresses me out.

It became my mission to book us all in Lufthansa first class, so I set out to read everything I could on Lufthansa award space. I became a Lufthansa award space sleuth and figured out not only the time of day that Lufthansa would release award inventory but when it would be available to their partners. The trickiest part was they would release them no more than two seats at a time, and often just a single seat. In a bid to remain flexible to heighten our chances, I was looking at multiple routes across 3 possible days. We just needed to get back into the US. We were going to a wedding in Phoenix a few days after our arrival, and we could easily get cheap flights to Phoenix wherever we reentered the US.

This is a pic of all us all dining on caviar and sipping ridiculously expensive champagne to finish off the trip. That flight could retail for $10,000 a ticket, and we did it for 240,000 miles and a few hundred in surcharges.

We were on the Asian section of our trip, at the Conrad Bali, when two Lufthansa first-class seats were released to Dallas on the A330. They not only released the long-haul section, but it left at a reasonable time from Nice and had a decent connection time at Frankfurt. I couldn't believe my eyes; I was sitting in the living room of my parents' suite when I saw it. I snuck out and phoned Singapore Airlines. Within minutes, I had paid the $20 change fee for each ticket, some additional surcharges, and locked up Lufthansa first class for my parents—Nice to Frankfurt to Dallas on the A330.

As soon as their seats were booked, I transferred 80,000 miles spread across Chase, Citi, and Amex into my Singapore account. Having those flexible points was clutch. I prayed that the miles would transfer closer to the 4 hours instead of the 48 hours. At some point the next day, Lufthansa released another first-class seat, and as luck would have it, my miles from all three banks populated my Singapore account by the end of the day, and I was able to book it. I didn't tell my parents this news. Instead, I told them that they were going to get to fly Lufthansa first class home, but the award space just didn't release for my ticket, and I'd have to fly separately. I went on to say that on the bright side, I was able to book business class on another airline so we could leave around the same time. I kept it a surprise until we were at the airport departing Cannes and we all checked in together. My performance would have made Christian Bale proud (as long as no one was making eye contact with me).

Having the ability to combine points from multiple flexible programs was great, but it would have been really difficult to earn the miles needed had we not been able to sign up for multiple credit cards bonuses across multiple programs. For the whole trip, between the three of us, we used over 500,000 Singapore miles. We were able to accumulate this many because we did it across multiple programs over a healthy period of time (12 to 18 months).

My long-term strategy is to always be accumulating points whenever possible. I have no idea what cool spot in some remote location I'll want to visit, or what airline will debut a new world class product that I'll be dying to try out. As long as I'm accumulating and diversifying the points I'm earning, I feel confident I'll be able to make something work in order to achieve those goals. Like anything in life, it's arduous when you're first starting out, but as you do it more, you get better at it, and the process becomes second nature.

On the next page is a list of all the programs and their transfer partners. This will undoubtedly change, but it should give you an idea of how many programs cross over and why it can be very beneficial to accumulate points across multiple programs.

"How do you know which flexible currency card to start with?"

Remember, you're wanting to build a main cast, and then over time you'll probably rotate and change your supporting characters. You can think of it as building different plotlines to your travel story :).

You want that main cast to accomplish the following things:

- Earn at least 1.5X flexible points on every purchase.
- Earn category bonus points.
- Keep your wallet uncomplicated.

The first step is to look at what cards are already in your wallet and the roles they fill. Do you have a card that lives in one of the flexible point ecosystems (Amex, Bilt, Brex, Capital One, Citi, or Chase), has a credit history, and is one that can be used in tandem with other cards? Or the reverse? Do you have a cash-back card that, if you added a premium card in tandem, you'd immediately increase the value of the points you currently have? Do you have any supporting characters like airline or hotel cards that you want to keep, but potentially pivot your main spending away from?

	Amex	Bilt	Brex	Cap One	Chase/Team Blue	Citi	Marriott
Total Partners	21	14	7	19	14	20	40
Aegean Airlines							Yes (3:1)
Aer Lingus	Yes	Yes			Yes		Yes (3:1)
Aeroflot							Yes (3:1)
Aeromexico	Yes		Yes	Yes		Yes	Yes (3:1)
Air Canada	Yes	Yes		Yes	Yes		Yes (3:1)
Air France/KLM Flying Blue	Yes	Yes	Yes	Yes	Yes	Yes	Yes (3:1)
Air New Zealand							Yes (200:1)
Alaska Airlines							Yes (3:1)
American Airlines		Yes					Yes (3:1)
ANA	Yes						Yes (3:1)
Asiana Airlines							Yes (3:1)
Avianca	Yes		Yes	Yes		Yes	Yes (3:1)
British Airways	Yes	Yes		Yes	Yes		Yes (3:1)
Cathay Pacific	Yes	Yes	Yes	Yes		Yes	Yes (3:1)
Copa Airlines							Yes (3:1)
Delta	Yes						Yes (3:1)
Etihad	Yes			Yes		Yes	Yes (3:1)
Emirates	Yes	Yes	Yes	Yes	Yes	Yes	Yes (3:1)
EVA Air				Yes		Yes	
Finnair				Yes			
Frontier Airlines Miles							Yes (3:1)
Garuda Indonesia						Yes	
Hainan Airlines							Yes (3:1)
Hawaiian Airlines	Yes	Yes					Yes (3:1)
Iberia Plus	Yes	Yes			Yes		Yes (3:1)
InterMiles							Yes (3:1)
Japan Airlines							Yes (3:1)
Jet Airways						Yes	
JetBlue	Yes			Yes	Yes	Yes	Yes (3:1)
Korean Air							Yes (3:1)
LATAM Airlines							Yes (3:1)
Malaysian Airlines						Yes	
Qantas	Yes		Yes	Yes		Yes	Yes (3:1)
Qatar						Yes	Yes (3:1)
Saudia Airlines							Yes (3:1)
Sears						Yes	
Singapore Airlines	Yes		Yes	Yes	Yes	Yes	Yes (3:1)
South African							Yes (3:1)
Southwest					Yes		Yes (3:1)
TAP Air Portugal				Yes			Yes (3:1)
THAI Airways						Yes	Yes (3:1)
Turkish		Yes		Yes		Yes	Yes (3:1)
United		Yes			Yes		Yes (3: 1)
Virgin Australia							Yes (3:1)
Virgin Red	Yes	Yes		Yes	Yes	Yes	Yes (3:1)
Vueling Club							Yes (3:1)
Hotel Partners							
Accor				Yes			
Choice Hotels	Yes			Yes		Yes	
Hilton Honors	Yes						
IHG Hotels	Yes	Yes			Yes		
Marriott	Yes				Yes		
World of Hyatt		Yes			Yes		
Wyndham				Yes		Yes	

I recently had someone ask me a question on Instagram regarding their Capital One miles. She had over 500,000 miles earned over many years and wanted to take a trip to Europe for a major anniversary. She wanted to know how to best use them. The problem? She had earned them on cards that only permitted redemption in the Capital One travel portal or cash back. So I mentioned that Capital One, like Chase and Citi, allows users to combine points between cards, and even though it's not advertised, her miles could become transferable if she simply added one of the Capital One products that earns flexible points to her wallet. She'd never even considered the idea, but was willing to experiment. She ended up choosing the Capital One Venture X card, since it offered a lot of additional travel perks they could make use of on her European trip, and it was offering a massive sign-up bonus. As suspected, once the new card was added to her account (shortly after approval), she was able to combine points and make use of transfer partners.

That was the best first card for her to get. She had supporting character credit cards, but what she was really missing was a main character that offered transferable points. By adding a single card, the value of her points nest egg was immediately improved upon.

I've had college grads reach out to me and ask what I think their first card should be. They just got their first job, are moving to a big city, and they want a great card. Most 20-somethings are first-time renters and spend a lot of money on dining and travel. The biggest question for them is this: Do you have any established credit history?

If the answer is no, then you're in the position whereby you'll have a job, solid income, you're educated, but there isn't anything to underscore your ability to pay back debt responsibly. This is a great opportunity to invert the option I gave above. Instead of adding a premium flexible point card to your wallet, pick up a cash-back card that is a part of a flexible point ecosystem. These are much easier to attain, and down the road, oftentimes within 6 to 12 months, you'll be able to add the premium card to your wallet and instantly improve the value of the points you've been earning since graduation. As you build your credit history and your score improves, you can go on to build a cast of cards that serve your goals.

When the answer to that question is yes, you want to consider two things:

- What flexible point card has a fantastic sign-up bonus?
- Can I earn points on my largest expense: rent?

Oftentimes, college grads have a credit history if they've been an authorized user on their parent's credit cards and have scores over 720. I'll point them toward flexible currency cards that align with their potential habits. If I were in that situation, or it had been roughly a year since graduating and I'd established a pretty solid credit score, I would take a close look at a company I'm an investor in: the Bilt Rewards Mastercard. Why? It has no annual fee, earns flexible points, has a travel and dining bonus category, and (drumroll) allows you to pay your rent with a credit card fee-free. It also reports your rent to credit agencies, thus helping your score. For this demographic, it's a super easy credit card to use that will earn them great points and build their credit history through the card and their rent. That's a win-win.

The biggest reason I would delay getting that card would be because another card is offering an all-time-high sign-up bonus, or one that breaches 100k. If you qualify for a flexible point card that is offering an all-time-high sign-up bonus, and it could serve as a main character of your wallet, that should draw a lot of your attention and focus.

Personally, I'd also look to add on two or three cards in the first 18 months after graduation that will earn flexible points and more than 1X on your base spending. The order depends on your credit history, the level of sign-up bonus when you're ready to apply, and whether you rent or not.

Most often, my top picks to pair with the Blit Rewards Mastercard are the Chase Sapphire Preferred as a main character with a supporting character of the Chase Freedom Unlimited. You'd be earning points on your rent; 1.5X on all your base spending; 2X on all travel; and 3X on all dining, online groceries, pharmacies, select streaming, and even Chase travel portal bonuses for hotel and flights booked there. In total, all three cards would cost just $95 in annual fees.

Every single situation is different, but where you should start relies heavily on your credit score, your current wallet situation, your short- and long-term goals, and the card offers you qualify for.

At this point, you should be feeling pretty spicy knowing that you have the skills to design a wallet that can really put in the hard work on your everyday expenses and get you closer to your goals. But we can't just stop there. I wrote a whole book, not a pamphlet, gosh dang it! If you really want to achieve those travel dreams, you need to not only have a wallet that serves your goals, you also need to understand all the ways you can earn points in tandem with the right credit cards.

HOW TO EARN POINTS
AND MILES

The number one question I get is, *"Zach, what's the best credit card?"* Hopefully by this point you can answer that one for me! I was never a fan of pop quizzes, so I'll go ahead and remind you :). There isn't one! As we now know, it all comes down to your goals and strategy. A big part of developing that ongoing strategy (one that you can tailor over time) relates to my very, very close number two question:

"How do you earn so many points?"

Welcome to the rabbit hole. When I first started down the travel hacking rabbit hole, I couldn't believe my eyes. Was this for real? How are there so many creative ways to earn points and miles to fund your travel hacking dreams? When I first started it, was still the Wild West. Banks had very lenient rules in terms of how often you could earn bonuses, the airlines had amazingly customer-friendly award charts and routing rules, the hotels had lower barriers to elite status, and if you were willing to drill, you could easily find oil. While the space isn't as fruitful as it once was, I'd say you can simply and effectively earn a few hundred thousand points a year without excessive labor.

Much of your ability to earn points hand over fist lies in the rules the banks lay out for you and how you can negotiate them. You want to be viewed as a profitable customer and have a good relationship that builds and secures your credit, but also maximize your ability to achieve your aspirational travel goals.

One rule that has consistently evolved over time is the sign-up bonus (aka the welcome offer, welcome bonus, or loyalty bonus) rule. Most people don't realize that you can get a welcome offer more than once, and every bank has a different rule associated with how frequently you qualify. These change. All. The. Time. In fact, it's not uncommon for a bank to "technically" keep a rule on the books only to circumvent their own rule via targeted offers. It's very beneficial to do a quick search to see what the updated rules are for each bank.

For instance, American Express currently has a "once in a lifetime" rule for new applicants applying to receive a welcome offer. Meaning, if you've ever gotten a welcome offer in "a lifetime" you can't get it again. But what's a lifetime? The assumption would be that it's YOUR lifetime, but in fact, it's the relative lifetime of how Amex views a credit cycle. If you had an Amex Platinum, closed it, and it's been more than 7 years, anecdotally it's quite likely you'd be eligible to get that welcome offer once again. So in the eyes of Amex, 7 years is a lifetime. Interesting, right? (I can think of some other words to describe this but will leave that to your imagination.)

Why is it so complex?

Points have become big business for banks, airlines, and hotels. Banks, like American Express, buy billions of dollars' worth of miles from airlines like Delta, United, and American Airlines, which in turn creates liquidity to finance their ongoing flight operations. As banks buy larger quantities of points, they increase their welcome offers, and points flood the accounts of loyalists. In turn, airlines then feel free to devalue their programs to absorb the excess supply. I won't comment whether this irritates the banks, since they purchased billions of dollars of those points only to see the airline diminish their value, but this is the cycle.

In fact, I'd go so far as to say that many, if not most, airlines lose money flying, and instead make their money from their respective loyalty programs. Banks loosen and tighten the welcome offer rules much in the same way a central bank will stimulate an economy with cheaper interest rates. If you need to stimulate demand, offer a really high welcome offer and stop enforcing the draconian sign-up bonus rules.

Years ago, American Express had a 12-month rule. Meaning, as long as you hadn't had the card in the prior 12 months, you could get it again. I didn't realize this for the longest time, but you could get a welcome offer on an Amex Platinum, keep it for 12 months, close it, and then on the 366th day (or 367th if in a leap year) apply for the card again and qualify for the welcome offer. That made earning points incredibly easy, especially if you were willing to hold more than one Amex card and rotate through them. As long as one Amex card was open, and it earned Membership Rewards, your points were safe and wouldn't expire.

Do I look as smug as I felt flying with a glass of champagne in my hand and a monkey on my shoulder? :)

Often rules are rewritten during transitional times of reorganization, acquisitions, or crises. This happened in 2015.

In 2015, American Airlines finalized the acquisition of US Airways. One impact of that acquisition was that anyone who had a US Airways account was converted into an American Airlines account, and the same thing happened to all the existing US Airways credit card holders.

See, US Airways had a contract with Barclays, and American Airlines had a longstanding deal with Citi. Anyone who had a Barclays US Airways credit card had their account immediately converted into a new product called the Barclays Advantage Aviator Red World Elite Mastercard that would earn American miles. It's highly unusual to see two banks issue credit cards that earn miles with the same airline, but again, rules are rewritten during transitional periods.

American Airlines negotiated a deal whereby Barclays could market their Aviator Red in-flight and within airports, and Citi could basically have everything else. As part of this new rollout, Barclays dropped an unheard-of offer: Earn 50,000 American miles after making a single purchase and paying the $89 annual fee. Literally one purchase plus $89 equals 50,000 miles. This was an insanely good deal at the time considering you could fly business class to Europe, South America, or Japan for that many miles.

Here's where knowing the rules of each bank is very, very handy.

Clearly I wanted to add the new Barclays Aviator Red to my wallet. I had newly started my blog and wanted to review as many business-class products as possible. My eyes widened and my mouth watered at how stupidly easy it was to generate 50,000 American Airlines miles after a single purchase. It was compounded by the fact that I had also used up a hefty portion of my American Airlines miles to fly the Etihad business studio for an African safari.

I needed to replenish my American Airlines balance for travel I was planning in 2016 to Europe and Southeast Asia. The Barclays deal coincided with an incredible offer from Citi as well. If you funded a new Citigold checking account, made $1,000 in debit transactions, and used bill pay for 2 consecutive months, they'd give you 50,000 American Airlines miles.

Seriously? Somebody pinch me!

I thought to myself, I'd love to earn an easy 50,000 miles from Barclays, but what if I could snatch the Citi banking bonus too? What were the rules I was working with at the time, and how could I use them to my advantage? Well, they were quite advantageous.

At the time, Citi allowed the funding of a bank account via a credit card. Do you see where this is going? I could use my Barclays Aviator Red to fund my Citigold account and trigger both offers. Barclays even credited bank funding as a normal point earning purchase, and, as long as you lowered your cash advance line down to $0, you didn't have to worry about a cash advance fee either.

Here's an email that I sent my buddy in 2015 that laid it all out:

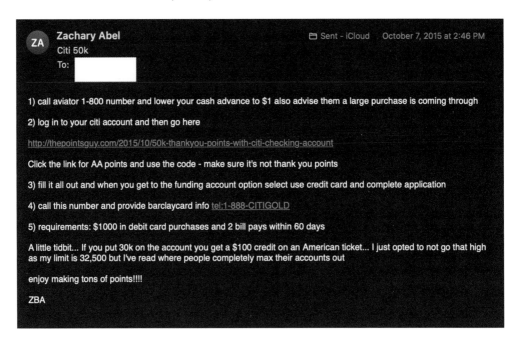

Zachary Abel
Citi 50k

Sent - iCloud   October 7, 2015 at 2:46 PM

To:

1) call aviator 1-800 number and lower your cash advance to $1 also advise them a large purchase is coming through

2) log in to your citi account and then go here

http://thepointsguy.com/2015/10/50k-thankyou-points-with-citi-checking-account

Click the link for AA points and use the code - make sure it's not thank you points

3) fill it all out and when you get to the funding account option select use credit card and complete application

4) call this number and provide barclaycard info tel:1-888-CITIGOLD

5) requirements: $1000 in debit card purchases and 2 bill pays within 60 days

A little tidbit... If you put 30k on the account you get a $100 credit on an American ticket... I just opted to not go that high as my limit is 32,500 but I've read where people completely max their accounts out

enjoy making tons of points!!!!

ZBA

Dave and I flying Japan Airlines First Class for the first time from Tokyo to Los Angeles

In the end, I funded the Citigold account with $25,000. That charge showed up on my Barclays Aviator Red as a qualifying point-earning purchase. I then immediately scheduled two bill pays on my Citigold account. What bill did I schedule? My Barclays Aviator Red. I owed $25,000 on my credit card and had $25,000 sitting in a Citigold account now that could be used to pay it off. How best to reallocate those funds to stay debt free? Go back to the rules.

To earn the 50,000 American Airlines miles from Citigold, I needed to:

- Spend $1,000 on debit transactions.
- Have two bill pays within 60 days.

Instead of paying off my credit card in full via a single payment, I scheduled two installments several days apart for $23,900. This was enough to fulfill the two bill payments I needed, but also left $1,100 in the account. So I'd have the funds to trigger the $1,000 debit card requirement. My landlord accepted debit payments for rent. So instead of writing a check, I simply paid $1,050 of my rent on my debit card and the remainder with a check. The $1,100 I still owed on my credit card I paid out of the account I'd have normally paid my rent from. I'm not saying this didn't take a little bit of work to achieve, but it was well worth it to me to earn that many points.

In the end, here's my total point haul plus cost:

- 125,000 American Airlines miles
    - » 50,000 offer via Barclays card
    - » 25,000 in spending on Barclays card
    - » 50,000 Citigold banking bonus
    - » $89 annual fee

Were you wondering what the miles ended up getting used for? Roughly a year later, at the end of 2016, I took a trip to Southeast Asia with my buddy Dave. The return from Vietnam was booked in first class on Japan Airlines for 67,500 American miles. It retails for over $10,000, which easily justified the work I put into earning those American Airlines miles!

WHAT ARE THE RULES?

Knowing the rules is an important part of the system. Of course, these are going to consistently evolve over time, but let's go through the basic rules of each bank, which will give you an idea of what to consider when you want to apply for a new card.

We are going to focus on six major banks. Here's the lineup.

- Chase
- American Express
- Citi
- Capital One
- Bank of America
- Barclays

This order is indicative of how I would rank the weight of each bank's application rules and how much impact the rules could have on building your wallet. For instance, Chase has a lot of really attractive cards and quite strict rules, which means you should pay a lot of attention to how they enforce and evolve these rules. Bank of America doesn't have a flexible points program and has a small number of cobranded cards, so I pay very little attention to their rules—excluding those for their Alaska Airlines cards, which I think are quite valuable.

As you read through the rules of each bank, you'll notice a trend, and hopefully it will prompt you to form strategic ideas relative to new card applications:

- Does the bank care how often you apply for any new cards regardless of the bank?
- Does the bank care how often you apply for the credit cards of that specific bank?
- How often does the bank deem you eligible to get a sign-up bonus?
- How many credit cards does the bank let you have at one time?
- Do Twinkies contain gluten? Oh wait, different list.

Chase

Chase is a great starting point for many beginners because their program is very straightforward and full of US domestic transfer partners that many users will recognize. Chase cards are also frequently on the short list of cards to sign up for first because of their restrictive application—mainly, the infamous five in 24 rule. What is it? How do you navigate it? We have the answers. Let's dig in so you have a clear idea of what to look out for when the time comes for you to apply for a Chase credit card.

Chase rules:
- Five in 24
- Two in 30
- 24-month rule
- Family rules
- Credit rotation plus reconsideration
- Unlimited cards

Five in 24

This is the most infamous credit card sign-up rule in existence.

This rule was implemented in 2016 when Chase rocked the credit card ecosystem with the release of the Chase Sapphire Reserve and challenged the Amex Platinum for best premium card on the market. It was a big moment, and Chase drew a line in the sand. Buried in the fine print of the application was wording to this effect:

"You will not be approved for this card if you have opened five or more bank cards in the past 24 months."

They soon pulled the language from applications, but behind closed doors, they kept the restriction in place. Over time, it's popped up on applications here and there, but it's never gone away, and it has become one of the most well-known credit card applications rules, bar none.

So what does this mean?

Chase usually won't approve anyone for a new card who has five or more new card accounts opened on their personal credit report in the prior 24 months. This applies to any bank, not just Chase, and notice that I say personal credit report. Most often business cards aren't reported to your personal credit report (there are exceptions, like Capital One, Discover, and Barclays), but that's the general rule. Banks will pull your personal report when you apply, but usually they will only report negative remarks and not all transactions. This means you could actually open more than five card accounts in the past 24 months, but it's only your personal cards that are reported.

Chase itself abides by this philosophy. Let's say you've opened four cards in the last 24 months. You'd be under the five in 24 limit, and therefore you would qualify for one of their business credit cards. However, if you were approved for one, that account wouldn't be added to your five in 24 number. Even though you opened it, your number would still be four in 24. If you're a small business owner, this is a great way to use the system to your benefit and accumulate business cards rather than personal ones to keep your five in 24 number low while racking up a lot of welcome offers.

Understanding five in 24 is imperative to your wallet strategy and for earning points. Chase has a great group of cards, and for years I've always tried to stay under the five in 24 limit just in case one of them has an incredible offer that I want to be able to sign up for. What happens if you see more than one offer that looks really appealing and you're under five in 24? Well, the next rule is one to keep in mind.

Two in 30
Chase will only approve two new accounts in a rolling 30-day period. This is pretty simple and straightforward. This applies to both personal and business credit cards.

24-Month Rule*
Chase permits you to get a sign-up bonus more than once on the same card, which is pretty awesome. For nearly all of their cards, you are ineligible for a new bonus if you received a bonus on that card in the prior 24 months. Now you can't sign up for that card and hold it, so you'd need to downgrade or cancel prior to reapplying. But if it's been longer than 24 months since the bonus populated in your account, you can get it again.

*A couple of years ago, Chase implemented a 48-month rule specifically for their Sapphire-branded cards. It's exactly the same rule as above, except it's 48 months since you received a sign-up bonus on any Sapphire-branded card (currently that's Preferred and Reserve).

Family Rules

These apply to:

- Sapphire-branded cards

- Southwest-branded cards

- IHG-branded cards

Chase took a page out of Citi's book (don't worry, we'll get to that) and imposed a family rule on certain cards. If you hold a personal version of any of the Sapphire cards, you can't hold any other Sapphire cards. Currently, there are only two, the Preferred and Reserve, but who knows what will happen in the future. We call those cards the Sapphire family.

The family rule applies to the Southwest- and IHG-branded cards as well. If you have any of the personal versions, you're automatically ineligible to add any of the other personal cards. This doesn't apply to the business versions of the branded cards, so you could technically have more than one Southwest card or IHG card, but it would have to be one personal and one business.

Credit Rotation plus Reconsideration

Chase allows you to rotate credit lines from one card to another without a hard pull on your credit. You can do this during the application process as well as once you become a cardholder. Let's say you get denied for the Chase Sapphire Preferred because the bank has given you as much credit as it can. Instead of taking no for an answer, Chase allows you to call their reconsideration department. So if you already hold a Chase IHG Premier card with a $20,000 line, you could call reconsideration and request that $10,000 from that IHG Premier line be moved to the Chase Sapphire Preferred in order to approve the card.

Some people have even been given this option electronically during the application process. Either way, this is a really great feature that Chase affords its applicants so they can add new cards to their wallet even if they've extended the maximum amount of credit. To get the number for reconsideration, just give it a Google and type it into the search bar. Unfortunately, I haven't found a reconsideration department for that time I consumed a whole packet of Life Savers.

What exactly is reconsideration? Reconsideration is the department of a bank within lending that allows you to contest your application, or at least allows you to request more information regarding your denial. Sometimes it's as easy as verifying information or rotating credit; other times it's because you didn't pay attention to one of the rules above, or they simply don't want to do business with you due to your credit or prior banking history. If I'm denied for a card, I always call the reconsideration department and ask for more information—this is how I uncovered many of these rules.

Unlimited Cards

Chase currently does not set a cap on the number of credit cards you can hold at any one time. You won't be denied simply for having too many open accounts, but I wouldn't push it. You want to maintain a healthy relationship with the banks you do business with, and also put some spending on your cards every year, or you could face having your account shut down for nonuse. Currently, I have nine and may up that to ten this year, depending on the offers. We shall see.

American Express

American Express has several application rules that you need to be aware of, and we will cover the most important ones that are currently being enforced. Amex is a bank that issues both charge cards and credit cards. Remember, charge cards need to be paid off in full every month whereas credit cards have a credit line attached to them and permit fractional payments over time

Sometimes when it's really hot outside I use my Chase cards as a fan ;).

with an interest rate assessed. Amex has some rules that only apply to their credit cards, so make sure you are paying attention to the distinction. There will be a test. (Just kidding. I'm your cool friend Zach.)

Amex rules:

- Credit cards vs. charge cards
- Once in a lifetime rule
- Five credit card limit
- Two in 90
- One in 5
- Clawbacks, exceptions, pop-ups, and targeted offers

Credit Cards vs. Charge Cards

Amex issues both credit cards and charge cards. If you've ever wondered why a lot of businesses don't accept American Express, it's because Amex has traditionally charged a higher "swipe fee" than other credit card networks. Why? Their history is rooted in the charge card system, which doesn't issue a line of credit that you can pay over time. Instead, you must pay them off in full every month. If you're paying the card off in full, the bank isn't collecting interest on your unpaid debt. They need to offset that income somehow, and they have traditionally done so via their payment network fees.

Amex keeps different rules for charge cards and credit cards, which I outline below.

Once in a Lifetime Rule

I discussed this earlier in the book, but American Express will only give a welcome offer once in a lifetime. This is per card and per cardholder. If you had the Amex Platinum credit card 4 years ago, canceled the card, and you wanted to get it again, you would most likely be ineligible for the welcome offer again.

A little reminder: anecdotally, a lifetime is 7 years of inactivity, meaning, if you closed a card more than 7 years ago, you're likely past the "lifetime" restriction and eligible to get a welcome offer again.

This rule applies to both charge cards and credit cards.

Five Credit Card Limit

Unlike Chase, which will theoretically permit you to hold an infinite number of credit cards, Amex caps you at five.

This rule applies only to credit cards, not charge cards.

Two in 90

Amex will approve you for a maximum of two credit cards in a 90-day period.

Again, this rule applies only to credit cards, not charge cards. (If I were a songwriter and my band was named Amex, this would be the chorus of our debut single.)

One in 5

Amex will only approve you for one credit card every 5 days. You may be thinking, *Zach, you said two cards in 90 days, now you're saying one in 5.* It works like this: you could get a credit card on May 1, but you'd need to wait until May 6 to get the second. Then you'd need to wait 91 days from May 1 if you wanted to add a third card, so that it would be outside the 90-day window of your first card. I did say we were going down into the rabbit warren.

Clawbacks, Exceptions, Pop-Ups, and Targeted Offers

If Amex deems that you've somehow manipulated or abused these rules, they reserve the right to clawback your bonus. Meaning, if you got the 150,000 Amex Platinum welcome offer, but you got a welcome offer just a couple of years ago, and so were actually ineligible but managed to skirt the system, they will take your points back and maybe even shut down your entire account.

You may be thinking, *Chamon, Zach, this never happens,* and you'd be wrong. I've known a lot of people who've had their bonuses clawed back without much explanation, and even some who were shut down. As a result of these clawbacks, Amex created a pop-up feature that will warn you if you're ineligible for a welcome offer.

"Zach, then how do you have so many Amex cards and multiple versions of each?"

Every rule has exceptions. With Amex, the biggest exception to the once in a lifetime rule is the "targeted offer." In the past couple of years, I've gotten a steady stream of them. Most often they are preapproved offers with no restrictive language and are either mailed to my home or sent to my email. These are targeted to me, and I regularly take advantage of them.

It's why I now have ten Amex cards and only two of them are credit cards (the two American Express Blue Business Plus cards). And yes, I got welcome offers on all of them.

Citi

Over the years, I've had a lot of Citi cards, and Citi has developed quite strict application rules. You'll notice the trend of rules that limit the rate at which you can add cards to your wallet continues, as well as repeat bonus limitations.

Citi rules:
- One in 8
- Two in 65
- 24-month rule
- Family rules
- One in 90 for business cards

One in 8

Citi will only approve you for one credit card every 8 days. If you try to apply for more, you'll get rejected.

Two in 65

Much like the one in 8 rule, you can only get approved for two cards every 65 days.

Day 1, get the first card. Day 9, get the second card (8 days later). Day 66, get the third card (65 days since the first card).

24-Month Rule

Good news: You can get a Citi sign-up bonus more than once on the same card, but you have to wait 24 months. Remember that Chase allows this as well and also has a 24-month rule. This one is very different. Whereas Chase starts the clock from when you get the bonus, Citi starts the clock from when you either cancel the card or change the product internally.

Month 1, get a Citi ThankYou bonus with a Citi Premier card. Month 13, downgrade the Citi Premier to a Citi Double Cash card. Month 27, you are now eligible for a Citi ThankYou bonus again!

Family Rules

When more than one card earns the same kind of points, we call that group of cards a family. Similar to the rules with Chase (regarding their IHG, Sapphire, and Southwest cards), Citi also has a family rule for cards that earn the same type of points. Of course, Citi adds nuance to their family rules by incorporating the 24-month rule. (They can't make it too simple now, otherwise, why would we need this book?)

- If you received a bonus in the past 24 months on a card that is within a family of cards, you're ineligible for a new bonus on another card in that family.
- If you canceled a card in the past 24 months that is within a family of cards, you're ineligible for a new bonus on another card in that family.

Let's say you received a welcome ThankYou bonus on the Citi Premier card and wanted to get a Citi Rewards + card. You'd need to wait 24 months to be eligible for the bonus on the Citi Rewards + card.

Yes, that is a custom outfit made for Miles by the lovely folks at Six Senses Maldives.

One in 90 for Business Cards

Citi will only approve you for one business credit card every 90 days.

Over the years, I've been fortunate enough to have the Citi trifecta. (So if you see me making a triangle with my hands at a rock concert, that's what I mean.)

The Citi trifecta:

- Citi Prestige: 5X dining
- Citi Premier: 3X air travel and hotels, dining, groceries, and gas
- Citi Double Cash: 2X unlimited, everywhere

Capital One

When I first dove down the rabbit hole, I didn't pay much attention to Capital One, since their entire program revolved around cash back. That all changed in 2018 when Capital One made a big splash with their transferable Capital One miles program. Ever since, they have continued to impress me, and understanding their rules has become a lot more important. But their rules aren't really clear at all. This is the only reason I rank them below Citi in terms of importance at this stage in the game. I see a lot of potential for Capital One going forward, and if their current trajectory persists, they'll be in the discussion for a top two program.

Capital One rules:
- One in 6
- Two personal cards
- Three bureau pulls

One in 6

Anecdotally, there is a rule, not strictly enforced, that you can only get approved for one card (personal or business) every 6 months. This was widely accepted as true until Capital One dropped the Venture X card at the end of 2021, and the rule completely fell apart. This is a great example of why these are things to keep an eye on, as they are constantly changing.

Two Personal Cards

Much like one in 6, it has long been understood that you couldn't have more than two Capital One personal cards. While this rule seems to hold for a lot of people, there are a lot of reports that it isn't universally enforced. Notice a theme? Capital One is shifting the program and the rules may, in fact, not even be rules anymore.

Three Bureau Pulls

Whenever you apply for a credit card, you normally have your credit report pulled from one bureau, but Capital One does it differently. Capital One will pull your report from all three bureaus. This seems to be quite consistently enforced. If you've applied for a lot of cards in the past year or two, or you're applying for more than one at a time, it could become a factor that affects your approval odds. Since Capital One is known to pull from all three bureaus, there's no hiding the number of applications or new lines of credit you've created, and, if they deem that risky, Capital One could reject your application.

It's also something to consider if you have a credit freeze with any of the bureaus, since you'll need to grant Capital One access to each via a thaw or pin.

Bank of America

I'll be the first to tell you that I haven't had much use for many Bank of America cards over the years. They've decisively stayed out of the transferable points game, which is where my focus has been. However, for every rule there is an exception. They have long been the issuing bank for Alaska Airlines credit cards, and Alaska Airlines miles are very valuable. For that single airline currency alone, I've held Bank of America cards from time to time. In fact, long, long ago, it was possible to apply for multiple Alaska Airlines cards on the same day. There were reports of people getting three, four, even five-plus of the same exact card on the same day. Let's just say, a rule was put in place quite quickly after multiple blogs reported on this feature.

Bank of America rules:
- Two/three/four/seven
- 24-month rule
- Five-card limit

Two/Three/Four/Seven

Bank of America cares most about how frequently you're adding their cards to your wallet. Perhaps it was a knee-jerk reaction to people getting so many of the same credit card at the same time. They throttled your ability to add cards by restricting the number you can add, and also imposed restrictions if you've added too many cards in general. The rules also change depending on whether you're a customer, and how much money you have.

Here we are enjoying caviar worth more than we paid in taxes for the ticket on the 14-hour Cathay Pacific flight from Hong Kong to LA. Smug.com/morecaviarplease.

Let's break down those numbers. Note they apply to personal/consumer cards:

- You can add two Bank of America personal cards in a 2-month period.

- If you have opened three new personal cards in a 12-month period, you will be denied if either you aren't a Bank of America customer or you have three cards from any bank that populates your personal credit report.

- If you have opened four new personal cards in a 24-month period, you'll be denied if you aren't a Bank of America customer or you have four cards from any bank that populates your personal credit report.

- If you've opened seven or more new personal cards in a 12-month period, you will be denied if you aren't a Bank of America customer or, if you are a customer (there are rumors this is not enforced), if you have more than $250,000 in assets.

24-Month Rule
Some Bank of America cards have a 24-month rule attached to them. This means that you're ineligible to open a Bank of America card and earn a welcome bonus if you've earned that bonus in the past 24 months or you currently hold the card.

Five-Card Limit
There is a five-card limit on how many Bank of America cards you can hold concurrently.

As I said, Bank of America has long been the issuing bank of the Alaska Airlines credit card. Just to show you how valuable Alaska Airlines miles can be, let me tell you a tale. I traveled to Australia in 2018, where my wife and I used Alaska Airlines miles to book one of the most incredible itineraries we have ever experienced. We flew Qantas first class from LA to Melbourne and Qantas business class from Melbourne to Sydney. After 2 weeks in Australia, we flew Cathay Pacific business class from Brisbane to Hong Kong, baked in a stopover for a few days, and then Cathay Pacific first class from Hong Kong to Los Angeles. The retail value of our flights was between $30,000 and $40,000 each, which we booked for 150,000 Alaska Airlines miles apiece. At the time, you could buy those miles for $2,400. How about that for a deal?

Barclays

Of the six issuers I'm covering, Barclays is the one I consider the least in my decision making. While rules pop up here and there, even before the pandemic, they were inconsistent at best. Since COVID-19? Who knows what's going on. Regardless, here are rules to be aware of if you ever consider adding a Barclays-issued card to your wallet.

Barclays rules:
- Six in 24
- Six months ago

Six in 24

Barclays won't approve you if you've had six or more cards added to your personal credit report in the past 24 months.

Six Months Ago

If you canceled a card more than 6 months ago, odds are, you're eligible for the welcome bonus again. This is a rule that had been quite reliable up until 2020, but since then, it's a shoulder shrug.

Recap

Once we know the rules, we can decide the order in which we may add cards to our wallet, or create "wallet flow." My wallet has a consistent main set of cards, but if I qualify for a bonus on those cards, I may reorganize my wallet temporarily to prepare to get another bonus.

I'm sure by this point you probably have a headache from all of these rules. Luckily, you can find the latest updates on my website. Most importantly, I hope this gives you insight into how you should be looking at the rules. Now let's look at how you can navigate the rules to earn the most points while staying within the lines. Let's get to hacking baybaaaaaaaay!

WELCOME OFFERS/SIGN-UP BONUSES

Bar none, there isn't a better allocation of your expenditures than using them to hit a minimum spending requirement and unlocking a sign-up bonus. So much of knowing the rules is geared toward taking advantage of those sweet, sweet sign-up bonuses as often as suits your goals. My goal is to help you hit the bull's-eye when you decide the timing is right and you pull the trigger. As you know, your credit will be affected, and after reading all those rules, who knows. It could be your only time getting that bonus for a long time, maybe ever. Not all sign-up bonuses are created equal.

Affiliate Links

Affiliate links are used by banking partners, like myself, to earn an income from the commission we're paid when you use our links. Those links direct you either to an affiliate partner website associated with the bank, or directly to the bank where you can apply for the card you want. When these are the best offers out there, it's a great way to support your favorite blogger.

However . . .

Here's a major heads-up, and one I try to explain on my site: these affiliate offers may not be the best offers you can get for yourself. Most websites will only publish the offers that make them a commission and won't mention or direct you to more attractive offers because they don't make any money from doing that. I've been very fortunate to build an audience that uses my affiliate links when they are the best available. I think those who enjoy my content have stayed loyal to me because I do my best to list the very best offers available, whether I make money from them or not. In fact, I do my best to get my audience in on the action by hosting referral pages for multiple credit cards, so they get the kickback from sign-ups. This has been particularly lucrative on Amex cards, since personal referrals have populated some of the best offers for affiliate links (like the ones I can offer) over the past couple of years. This means that readers who leave their links on my site are able to earn points referring other readers to great card offers. It's a win-win.

No blogger is perfect, everyone misses an offer, but some do a much better job than others at highlighting best available offers rather than just showing the links that earn them a commission. I urge you to spend a few extra minutes prior to applying to ensure you're getting the best deal for yourself.

One of the easiest ways to see if you're targeted for a better offer is circumventing the cookies placed on your computer.

Incognito/Private Browser Mode

It's like a magic button. Click it and see if your welcome offer magically improves. Here's how it works. Whichever browser you're using, if you go to "File" and look at the drop-down menu, you'll see either "Private browser" or "Incognito"—this will open your browser without the cookies embedded on it.

An example on Safari:

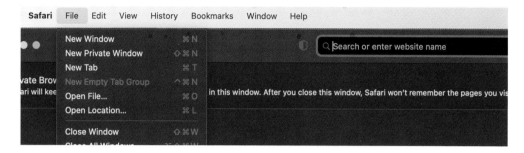

An example on Chrome:

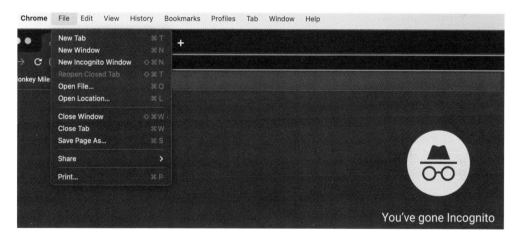

You may know that banks drop cookies on your computer every time you visit the site, but you may not know that those cookies will dictate the offer you get from them. By going through a private browser, without the cookies, you are able to populate different offers. This strategy works on referral offers as well.

American Express Gold Referral 60k to 90k Offer after $4k in 6 months

This is what most are getting...

American Express® Gold
Card

AMERICAN EXPRESS
C.F.FROST

Enjoy 4x points at restaurants worldwide‡

Annual Fee $ 250□†

LIMITED TIME REFERRAL OFFER

REFERRAL OFFER

Earn 60,000 Membership Rewards® Points

after you use your new Card to make $4,000 in purchases within your first 6 months of Card Membership. Plus, for a limited time if you apply for this Card by 06/08, you can receive 20% back as a statement credit on eligible purchases made on the Card at restaurants worldwide up to $250 back during the first 12 months of Card Membership.†

APR for Pay Over Time Feature

15.99% to 22.99% variable APR on eligible charges.□

But some are getting this insane offer.

You can see here, very different referral offers

American Express® Gold
Card

AMERICAN EXPRESS
C.F.FROST

Enjoy 4x points at restaurants worldwide‡

Annual Fee $ 250□†

LIMITED TIME REFERRAL OFFER

REFERRAL OFFER

Earn 90,000 Membership Rewards® Points

after you use your new Card to make $4,000 in purchases within your first 6 months of Card Membership. Plus, for a limited time if you apply for this Card by 06/08, you can receive 20% back as a statement credit on eligible purchases made on the Card at restaurants worldwide up to $250 back during the first 12 months of Card Membership.†

APR for Pay Over Time Feature

15.99% to 22.99% variable APR on eligible charges.□

Often personal referrals will populate different offers based on the cookies on your computer. The 60k shown up top was populated based off the cookies on my computer. When I opened the same referral via Incognito (no cookies), the 90k offer populated.

Referrals

Referral offers can not only be an incredible way to generate points by referring your friends and family to your favorite credit cards, but it can also be a great way to find the best deals. As I mentioned before, my site will allow you to leave your referral links in the comments section of dedicated posts. This increases the chances that you will not only earn a referral bonus yourself, but the community also will be alerted as to what the best offers are in general. It's always worth researching what the best referral offer is on a card you're looking at adding. Just like any other offer, these can vary based on the person as well.

Keep an eye on the USPS! Some of the best offers come via snail mail.

If you're wondering why referrals will sometimes populate better offers than on a bank's website or through an affiliate, I'd surmise it has to do with customer acquisition cost. A referral is far cheaper for the bank than them paying to market cards, and therefore they can afford to give more points through these offers.

Referrals can be a great way to earn points from cards that you already possess or to get better welcome offers.

It's worth pointing out that you may get targeted for offers that are far better than what is publicly available.

Targeted Offers

Since your data is bought and sold on a regular basis on the Internet, it shouldn't come as a surprise that your behavior as a consumer is quite well known by marketers. If you've recently opened a business, moved, started buying baby clothes, or bought a new car, you'll not only receive targeted ads on your computer, but you'll also get targeted credit card offers.

These targeted offers can come when you're looking to buy an airline ticket and you're logged into your account—you may receive an email with preapproved language. And snail mail is still quite frequently used to target individuals with offers that aren't publicly available.

These are well worth paying attention to.

Targeted offers can be a great way of circumventing the sign-up bonus rules that we spoke about earlier. This has happened many a time to me, and I'm always combing through my mail, junk mail folder, and clutter to make sure I didn't miss any.

Targeted offers are how I've ultimately accumulated ten American Express cards and earned several hundred thousand points in the past year. Throughout the pandemic, Amex was incredibly aggressive at targeting small business owners with really attractive welcome offers, even on cards that they already had in their wallets. As you may recall, Amex only allows a welcome offer once in a lifetime. But one of the ways of bypassing that rule is through, yep, a targeted offer.

The easiest and fastest way to earn a heap of points or miles is via the welcome offer. But how do you earn major points when you're in between signing up for new cards? The biggest thing you want to create with your wallet is the ability to multiply the points earned on your regular everyday spending.

Getting the Same Card Again

One of the ways to continue to earn heaps of points is to get a card that you already have . . . again. Let's say you had the Barclays Aviator Red a few years ago. It's issued by Barclays, you cross-reference the latest bank rules, and you see that, hey, I can get this bad mamma jamma again. So you do. I regularly do it, and often it'll be the case that I still have the card in my wallet. One way you can advantageously use the rules to your benefit is to downgrade a card to another no-annual-fee card, and then apply for the card you downgraded.

One example of this would be the Chase Sapphire Preferred. As we just learned, the Sapphire cards require 48 months between sign-up bonuses. If you hit 48 months, and you'd like to get the latest offer, you could downgrade that Sapphire Preferred into a Freedom Flex or Freedom Unlimited, wait until the system shows the product change, and then reapply for the Sapphire Preferred. This would keep your old lines of credit open, your payment history intact, and you could add to your point balance.

Multiplayer Mode

I have consulted with many couples on the right way to handle credit cards. Should each person become an authorized user? Should each person have their own account? The answer to both questions is usually, yes!

Being a dynamic duo is super advantageous for accumulating points. Why? For starters, you can get the sign-up bonus on every card twice, but second, and more importantly, each person is keeping their individual credit scores healthy and active. If you're just an authorized user on someone's card and they remove you, it could give you a substantial hit to your credit score. If you're keeping your own lines of credit open and healthy, you're ensuring your future self has a great credit score.

"Points are my love language. Can we move them between accounts?"

I get this question a lot! (The part about the moving of points between accounts, not what my love language is. Although I think you could guess: points.) It really depends on the bank. For instance, Capital One allows you to move points between *any* Capital One account, regardless of whether the account you're moving the points to is a partner, child, spouse, or household member. Others, like American Express, don't allow any combining of points. Chase splits the difference and allows customers within the same household to merge.

These rules change all the time.

One work-around is incorporating authorized users. Usually when you add an authorized user, you can transfer bank points into their award accounts. For instance, if Elizabeth and I wanted to book awards flights on Air France to Paris next year, we'd be looking to use the American Express Flying Blue program for our tickets. My wife and I are authorized users on each other's cards. So if my wife had a bunch of Chase points and I had a bunch of Amex points, but not enough in either account to book two tickets, we could do this: My wife could move her Chase points into her Air France account, and since my wife is an authorized user on my Amex, I could add her Flying Blue account to my profile and transfer my Amex points into her Flying Blue account. This circumvents the restriction Amex has on combining points, and we could populate the Flying Blue account with enough miles for both tickets.

EVERYDAY SPENDING

At a minimum, you absolutely need to create the ability to earn 1.5X to 2X points per dollar on the purchases you make every day. This is something I've touched on throughout the book, but if you really want to squeeze out every point, and make your travel goals more attainable, I'd highly suggest looking at how category bonuses can be used in ways you may not first realize. Let's investigate.

Category Bonuses

A category bonus is simply when your card offers an increased rate of return when you spend money on certain categories like gas, dining, supermarkets, travel, and streaming. Not only do I urge you to figure out where you spend the most and get a card that offers a category bonus, but I would also strongly advocate you thinking outside the box on these categories as well.

For instance, let's say you have an Amex Gold which earns 4X on dining and 4X on US supermarkets up to $25,000 a year. Most people don't spend $25,000 a year at supermarkets, but you know what's really cool? Supermarkets sell gift cards to a wide variety of places, including Amazon. Ordinarily, if you spend a lot at Amazon with your Amex Gold (I'm really talking to Elizabeth here), you're only earning 1X points per dollar. Instead, what you could do is buy Amazon gift cards at the grocery store to trigger the 4X category bonus then load those onto your Amazon account. Suddenly, you're earning 4X points at Amazon.

Promotional Offers

Chase, Amex, Citi, and Capital One all advertise promotional offers for their cardholders. Currently, American Express has the most lucrative with their Amex Offers program that populates on your login screen, but many banks have them. It's worth looking at these on a monthly basis, because they not only save you money (spend X dollars to get X dollars in statement credit) and earn you big-time bonus points (spend X dollars to get X amount of points), but you could strategize around them to fit your time frame.

Let's say you fly quite a bit with Delta and a Delta offer populates in your Amex Offers but you don't need to book a flight right now. One technique I have employed is to read the terms and understand what will trigger the offer as a qualifying purchase, because you may still be able to take advantage of it. For example, in the fall of 2021 Amex had a great deal with Delta. It stipulated that as long as your purchase was done online via Delta.com or the Delta app, you could spend $300 and get $125 back as a statement credit. This meant you could go to Delta.com and buy a gift card and get $125 back. Suddenly, your future flight was cheaper, and if you didn't want to keep that gift card, you could always look into selling it on eBay.

Delta Amex Offers

❷ Spend $300 or more get $125 back
❷ Must be by 12/31/21
❷ Must originate in the US
❷ Must be purchased in USD
❷ Must be done online, via the Delta App, or the US reservation phone line
  ❷ valid on: airfare, fare upgrades, seat fees, bag fees, standby fees, and Delta Sky Club membership
❷ See exclusions below

∨ ▲DELTA	Spend $300 or more, get a $125 statement credit	EXPIRES	Redeem Now
	Delta Air Lines	12/31/2021	

DETAILS
Get a one-time $125 statement credit by using your enrolled Card to spend a minimum of $300 in one or more transactions direct with Delta Air Lines by 12/31/2021. Flight must originate in the U.S. and purchase must be in USD. See terms for exclusions.

Don't sleep on Amex Offers. Loads of points and $$$$ to be saved/earned.

Often if you have more than one card with a bank, you'll find it phrased differently on each card. Perhaps on one it will say "spend $300, get $125 back," but on another, you'll see "spend $300, get 12,500 American Express Membership Rewards." The second is an even better opportunity since Amex points are worth far more to me than a penny per point.

Tick. Tick. Tick. (That's my brain cogs turning.)

What if you could stack that Delta Amex deal to earn even *more* points? Sure, you could use an Amex Platinum and make a purchase directly with an airline and earn 5X points. But what if you first started your purchase at a shopping portal? Unfamiliar with shopping portals? Oh, just you wait.

SHOPPING PORTALS

This is not only going to completely change how you shop, but it is the easiest, most straightforward way to earn a ton of points or cash back on most of the purchases you make online. I know, that probably sounds like hyperbole. But seriously, it's so simple, and once you do it, you'll never look back. (Except maybe to take a selfie of the new jeans you bought online while also earning lots of points. I've been doing extra squats lately.)

Shopping portals code your online purchases to earn points or cash back simply by starting your online shopping journey at the portal's home page. They have become so popular that most of the big brands you'd ordinarily shop at will be affiliated with one, and you can easily earn a big point multiple on your purchases.

"Waaaait, wait, wait. Zach, I have no idea what you're talking about, what is an example of a shopping portal?"

Loads of airlines have shopping portals, some hotels do as well, and even some banks. Let's take a look at one from Alaska Airlines. As you can see in the Alaska Airlines Mileage Plan portal on the next page, there are a bunch of familiar names listed in the portal with an "Earn X miles per X dollars spent" next to them. If you started your online shopping there, you'd earn Alaska Airlines miles on your purchase alongside the points that your credit card earns. Magical right? And. So. Easy.

"Okaaaaay. Can you give me an example of how they work?"

If you're wanting to buy a new pair of Nikes, and Nike.com happens to have the best price, you'd want to start your purchase at a shopping portal to earn more points per dollar. Now let's say you wanted to earn Alaska Airlines miles more than any other award currency. You could start your order there and earn "3 Alaska Airlines miles on every dollar you spend on Nike.com." Once you click that button, you'll always see a message telling you that you're being rerouted to the website. Your order is now coded to earn Alaska Airlines miles via a cookie that is dropped on your computer. Easy as apple pie, which you could probably buy through a portal.

Notice that not all purchases will trigger the portal bonus, so always read those exclusions to ensure that the items you're purchasing are going to earn you the bonus intended.

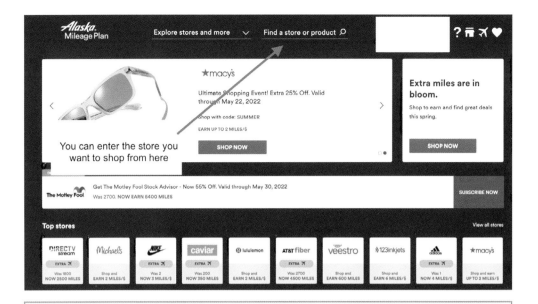

You can enter the store you want to shop from here

You're on your way to Nike!

one moment please

Place an order now, and you will earn 3 miles/$.

It's that simple.

Thank you for shopping through Mileage Plan™ Shopping.

Please note these terms & conditions: Not eligible on Hurley or Converse. Not eligible on Hurley wetsuits, flash sale items, Air Jordan Retros or other Jordan products. Not eligible on adjustments, reorders, non-US orders, purchases made on employee website, purchases made through the SNKR app, or orders deemed by Nike to be used for reselling purposes. Any return, exchange or other adjustment made at a physical store location for an online purchase may result in your purchase being deemed ineligible [...] with student, military, first responders or birth[day] purchases made with coupon or discount [...] Not eligible on gift cards, gift certificates [...] Purchases made with a gift card may be i[...]

Always look at the exclusions

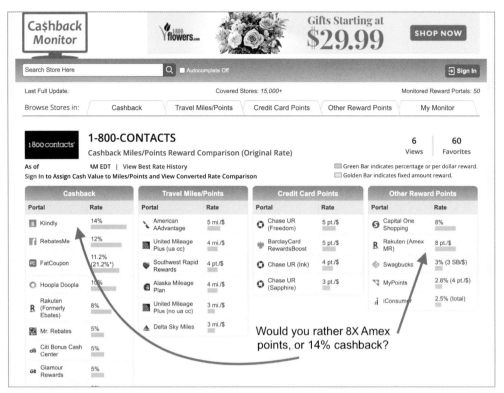

Search Store Here 🔍 ☐ Autocomplete Off   ⬦ Sign In

Last Full Update: Covered Stores: 15,000+   Monitored Reward Portals: 50

Browse Stores in: Cashback   Travel Miles/Points   Credit Card Points   Other Reward Points   My Monitor

1-800-CONTACTS
1800 contacts   6 | 60
Cashback Miles/Points Reward Comparison (Original Rate)   Views | Favorites

As of   AM EDT | View Best Rate History   ▨ Green Bar indicates percentage or per dollar reward.
Sign In to Assign Cash Value to Miles/Points and View Converted Rate Comparison   ▨ Golden Bar indicates fixed amount reward.

Cashback		Travel Miles/Points		Credit Card Points		Other Reward Points	
Portal	**Rate**	**Portal**	**Rate**	**Portal**	**Rate**	**Portal**	**Rate**
Kiindly	14%	American AAdvantage	5 mi./$	Chase UR (Freedom)	5 pt./$	Capital One Shopping	8%
RebatesMe	12%	United Mileage Plus (ua cc)	4 mi./$	BarclayCard RewardsBoost	5 pt./$	Rakuten (Amex MR)	8 pt./$
FatCoupon	11.2% (21.2%*)	Southwest Rapid Rewards	4 pt./$	Chase UR (Ink)	4 pt./$	Swagbucks	3% (3 SB/$)
Hoopla Doopla	10%	Alaska Mileage Plan	4 mi./$	Chase UR (Sapphire)	3 pt./$	MyPoints	2.8% (4 pt./$)
Rakuten (Formerly Ebates)	8%	United Mileage Plus (no ua cc)	3 mi./$			iConsumer	2.5% (total)
Mr. Rebates	5%	Delta Sky Miles	3 mi./$				
Citi Bonus Cash Center	5%						
Glamour Rewards	5%						

Would you rather 8X Amex points, or 14% cashback?

Cashback Monitor is my go-to before any online purchase.

"I'm interested, but how do I know which portal earns me the most points?"

So glad you asked! There is an excellent resource called cashbackmonitor.com that aggregates a ton of online shopping portals. I'm not sure that they list every single one out there, but they do a darn good job of capturing the big ones, and I reference it regularly.

For instance, if you wanted to buy eye contacts and 1-800-CONTACTS was offering you the best deal, you could search on cashbackmonitor.com to see which portal offers you the most cash back/points/miles per dollar on your purchase. There is a little bit for everyone. You could go cash back, fixed points, or flexible points. Which would you choose?

One thing to consider is the value of the points you're collecting. This is subjective and is dictated at the margin of consumer behavior. In other words, how you value each option may change depending on your goals at the time of your purchase. Perhaps you need the Alaska Airlines miles to tip you over the threshold for a Cathay Pacific booking for your

first trip to Asia. So even if the American portal was offering more miles per dollar, or Kiindly had more cash back, using the Alaska Airlines portal would serve your immediate goal and earn you the miles you need for your trip. So a fewer total number of points may actually be more valuable to you since they push you over a threshold needed for a desired booking.

If this is you, I feel ya! Alaska Airlines miles can be great! I've used them to fly Cathay Pacific business class on several occasions.

I'd rather earn flexible points than fixed-currency points unless there are extenuating circumstances, or if I could earn a lot more of the fixed-currency than the flexible currency (for example, if American is offering 15X compared to Chase offering 2X).

Here's a quick pic of me flying business class from Boston to Hong Kong on my mom's around-the-world trip in 2017. They flew first class while I slummed it in business class ;).

"I'm 100 percent onboard with shopping portals, but do they earn me elite status?"

The answer will continue to evolve over time. In 2021, American Airlines announced they were overhauling their entire loyalty program and making it completely spending based. As a result, the miles you earn through their SimplyMiles shopping portal qualify for American Airlines elite status.

My hunch is that many other programs will follow American Airlines' lead by redefining loyalty to become more spending based. In the past, loyalty was correlated to how much time you spent in an aircraft measured by miles or segments. Going forward, I suspect that loyalty will be redefined to correlate more closely to profit. If you're more profitable, you're considered more loyal, and you'll be rewarded with elite status.

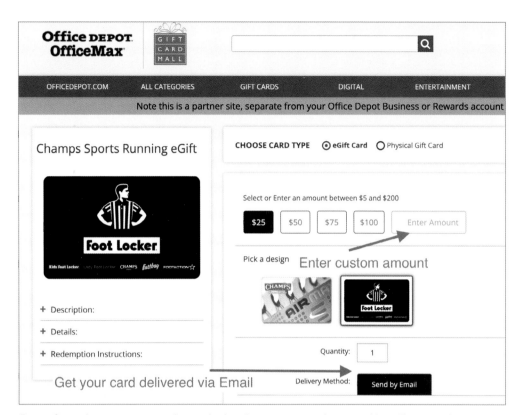

Buy gift cards using your credit cards that have category bonuses like office supply stores or supermarkets.

Shopping portals create more profit for the airline by selling miles indirectly to you. How? When you purchase through a shopping portal, the brands reimburse the portal with a percentage of the final sale as a commission. The portal then remits a portion of that to you, the consumer. If you choose cash back, the portal is splitting its profit from the sale with you. If you choose miles, the portal is using the portion of the commission that it would have given you as cash back to buy the miles from the airline. The portal effectively works as an intermediary for you to buy miles indirectly from the airline in lieu of getting cash back.

"Would I earn points if I'm using a gift card through a portal?"

Yes, in fact, this is a way that you could earn even MORE points. (Are you about ready to get a "shopping portal" tattoo yet?) Let's say you want those Nikes, but you realize that Foot Locker actually has the best deal. Here's what you could do. If you hold a Chase Ink Business Cash card, you earn 5X points at office supply stores. What on earth does an office supply store have to do with shoes?

Well, instead of going to Footlocker.com first, what you could do is go to OfficeDepot.com and search the 'gift card mall'. As luck would have it, they sell Footlocker gift cards. You can buy a gift card in the amount of the shoes that you want to purchase and earn 5X points on that gift card since it was purchased at an office supply store. The best part? A lot of gift cards can be delivered via email, so you don't even need to wait to take physical delivery.

From there, you'd go to cashbackmonitor.com and find which portal is offering the most points per dollar and redeem your gift card. Pretty slick, right?

Shopping portals are a super easy way to earn a lot of points per dollar that you'd miss if you were going straight to the retailer, or shopping in store.

But what happens if you are getting welcome offers when you can, maximizing your category bonuses, using shopping portals, and you're still falling short of the points required for a trip? My dear, you can buy points to push you over the top.

BUYING POINTS

In the fall of 2020, right after I had a root canal, I quickly posted on TikTok about the arbitrage opportunity of buying points. My jaw was sore, I wasn't articulating well at all, and I thought it'd be a quick, fun video to keep my daily streak alive. I had no idea it would go viral and that so many people were unaware of a simple truth: There are times when you can simply buy points to book flights cheaper than the cash rate. It seems hard to believe, but it's true! Let's dig into it and flesh out when you should take the plunge on buying points and when you should pass.

"When does buying points make sense?"

There are two major instances when it makes sense to buy points:

- When you don't have enough in your account to make a booking
- When the price to buy points is cheaper than the cash rate to buy the product

I've been in the situation quite a few times where I have been short on miles and needed to boost my account balance to the required booking amount. For instance, in 2018, when my wife and I flew to Australia in Qantas first class and then routed back through Hong Kong in a combo of business and first class on Cathay Pacific, it required 150,000 total Alaska Airlines Miles. My account had the needed miles, but my wife's account was short. Luckily, Alaska Airlines was selling their miles with a 40 percent bonus, or roughly 2 cents a point, which meant we could simply purchase enough miles to get her balance up 150,000 miles in order to book the flights.

One thing to keep in mind if you're in this position is whether you could book the award tickets via a different program. In our situation, we could have done so, but as I blogged about on my site, look at the difference in pricing by program for just the LA to Sydney portion of the ticket.

- Alaska Airlines is 70,000 miles.
- American Airlines is 110,000 miles.
- British Airways is a whopping 200,000 miles (and that would have only gotten us to Melbourne—we ultimately laid over there before connecting to Sydney).
- Cathay Pacific is 120,000 miles.
- Japan Airlines is 135,000 miles.
- Qantas is a staggering 325,000 miles.

Sure, we could have transferred points to several of those programs from Amex, Citi, or Chase, but the opportunity cost was very high. Why would I transfer 120,000 Amex points to Cathay Pacific for the first leg when I could spend under $1,000 to buy the points I needed to make the entire trip work? If I can buy miles to shore up my account to book a ticket, and the cost is reasonable, I can save the transferable points I have for a future trip when buying points isn't an option. While it may cost me a bit more money in the short term, over time, I will be able to travel in style more times for a reduced cost rather than blowing the points all at once.

This philosophy is why I've bought points when it's cheaper than the cash rate.

One great example of where this works really well is on high-end hotels. My wife and I celebrated the end of her TV show, Marvel's *Agents of S.H.I.E.L.D.*, with a trip around the world. (My wife jokes it was our show, since I played her one-night stand who she never called back in one of the deleted scenes.) Our second stop was Bali, where we met up with another couple. They opted for an Airbnb, and we chose to stay at the Alila Villas Uluwatu.

I'd long heard about Alila, and Hyatt had just purchased the brand not long before our trip. Alila, if you're unfamiliar, is an uber luxury hotel. The base room was over $1,000 a night and came with its own plunge pool. The best part? It was available for only 30,000 Hyatt points. Say whaaat? We were looking to stay 5 nights and had a decision to make: Do we transfer over Chase points to populate my Hyatt account with enough points for the booking, or do we buy points to cover a couple of the nights?

At the time, Hyatt was running a promo where you could buy Hyatt points for 1.7 cents. That $1,000 a night villa was 30,000 points, meaning we could buy nights at the hotel for $510, nearly half the cash rate.

The other thing we considered was what we would be sacrificing by using the Chase points rather than buying the Hyatt points. There is opportunity cost every time you use points, and typically I'm able to redeem Chase Ultimate Rewards for more than 1.7 cents apiece. In fact, earlier in 2022 we used 60,000 Chase points to book a one-way business-class flight to England by transferring the points to United. That flight would have easily been $2,000, or more than 3 cents per point.

So what did we choose? My Hyatt account had some points already in it, and we decided to transfer enough Hyatt points over to get the balance up to 90,000. We bought the other 60,000 points for $1,020. I looked at it like we were staying for 18,000 points plus $200 per night. Not bad for what would have been a $5,000 to $6,000 checkout bill.

"Are there times when I shouldn't buy points?"

Absolutely.

You shouldn't buy points unless you have a purpose for them. If Hilton is selling points and it's the best deal they've ever had, it still doesn't mean you should go for it. Airlines and hotels are notorious for changing their award pricing in the dead of night. I used Hilton for a reason. They sell points for 0.5 cent apiece *all the time*. I've written about it extensively and highlighted it on social media, but I do so with a biiiiig disclaimer. Don't buy them just because they are on sale. Buy them because you have a redemption you'd like to make, and this will fulfill it. I'd hate for you to buy points only to see their value diminish before you get a chance to use them.

"Can I get a recap?"

The biggest variable in your decision about whether to buy points comes down to value. I clearly valued keeping my Chase Ultimate Rewards for a future use and chose to buy points to offset my Alila stay. That may not be the case for you. Perhaps you don't want to spend any money, or you're sitting on millions of points you've accrued from work, and you're not concerned with squeezing out every last penny of value. At the end of the day, you want to buy points when it makes financial sense and fits into your overall strategy.

EARNING ELITE STATUS

Elite status is one of the easiest ways to accumulate and supercharge your points and miles. It will give you bonuses on the number of points you'd earn per stay, mile, or dollar; it'll get you upgrades to better cars, airline seats, or suites at hotels; and elite status may even grant you access to exclusive lounges in airports and hotels around the world. Sounds great right? In the words of my eight-year-old niece, "Yes but . . . ," the traditional pathway to elite status requires a lot of time and money spent on a single brand. There is a lot of competition between brands these days, and I find myself asking this question:

"Is elite status really worth it to me?"

The answer comes down to how much it costs to extract the benefits from elite status and the value you place on those benefits. Most often, elite status is achieved by money and time spent with a specific brand. However, there are a lot of pathways to elite status that circumvent you spending your time flying in the air or sleeping in a hotel bed. Arguably this lowers the cost associated with extracting those benefits.

Let's walk through how you could ascertain elite status in ways you may have never considered. After all, if you can earn points faster and add value to your experience when you redeem your points, you may be open to employing imaginative methods of achieving elite status.

Benefits of Elite Status

Before we get into the process of unlocking easier ways to achieve elite status, it would behoove us to understand why exactly we want elite status in the first place. Here are a few examples as to why you'd want to achieve it.

- Elite status will award bonus points on every dollar you spend with the brand. The higher the bonus points, the higher your status.
- Elite status unlocks perks such as upgrades, lounge access, free breakfast, free bags, and better seats. This is often true not just with the brand you achieve it with, but with their partners as well.
- Oftentimes you can match one elite status to another brand.
- Elite status has exclusive numbers to call for better, faster service.

"OK, my appetite has been whetted. How do I earn elite status without spending a load of dollars with the brand?"

Credit Cards for Elite Status

What if I told you that you never had to put your butt on a plane, put your head on a pillow, or suffer another airport car rental experience and you could still get elite status?

Yes, that's right. Credit cards can provide a pathway to elite status and, believe it or not, grant you elite status as a benefit of the card. Sure, achieving elite status via a credit card will cost you an annual fee, but it could be sizably cheaper than flying in planes, renting cars, or sleeping in hotel rooms. Elizabeth and I have several credit cards that we only keep in our wallets because they make it far easier to achieve elite status.

Credit Cards that Create Pathways to Elite Status

There are many cards that will create an easier pathway to achieving elite status. The principal way these cards grease the skids is by granting you a fixed number of elite qualifying nights, miles, dollars, or points. These are different from the points and miles you earn that can be used for future travel, and instead only count toward qualifying for elite status.

Depending on the card, you may receive these elite credits simply by keeping the cards in your wallet, or you may be awarded them by hitting a spending threshold. For instance, my wife and I have a Chase Marriott Bonvoy credit card, and every year it populates my wife's Marriott account with 15 elite nights. That means that without putting her head on a pillow, she has 15 elite nights already in her account. Elite nights are virtual stays that count toward elite status. I keep two credit cards that give my IHG One Rewards Platinum elite status simply by keeping the card in my wallet. Many airline credit cards will award you elite miles when you spend a certain amount of money on the card.

So what are these elite credits worth to you?

If you don't travel often, or you spread your travel across many brands, these elite credits are probably not worth a lot. But let's say you stay in Marriott hotels 15 to 20 nights a year. You would be considered a casual business traveler and far from a road warrior. Fifteen to 20 nights wouldn't do a lot for you in terms of Marriott elite status, since the best benefits start at Platinum status, which requires 50 elite nights or stays at the hotel. Well, if you had both an Amex and a Marriott-branded credit card, you'd earn 30 elite nights a year. Suddenly, the annual fees you're paying have paved the road to a very valuable elite status that comes with elite points bonuses, free breakfast, lounge access, and suite upgrades.

We enjoyed a comped breakfast at the Waldorf Dubai, a perk of our Amex Hilton Honors Aspire credit card.

Everyone will value these benefits differently, but crunching the numbers on the annual fees would be well worth your time.

Most of the cards that pave the way to elite status are what I consider to be supporting players to your wallet. Traditionally they only earn points or miles in the program they are affiliated with and are best used to extract benefits like elite credits to aid your travel. They aren't the cards I'd advocate putting the bulk of your spending on, but they could be advantageous when using them on the brand.

Credit Cards that Yield Complimentary Elite Status

My wife and I hold several cards that offer complimentary elite status as a benefit of holding the card. We don't have to spend anything to keep the compensated status; we just pay the annual fee and the elite status is given. This would be the case with the American Express Platinum and Business Platinum, as they have long extended Marriott and Hilton midtier status as a benefit of the card. While these midtier status levels earn bonus points, upgrades from time to time, and maybe even small dining perks, they don't change your experience at a hotel substantially. Most of the cards that offer a compensated status come with a bevy of other perks that, when analyzed in aggregate, easily outweigh the annual fee of the card.

However, you want to keep your eye out for unicorn offers. ("Unicorn offers" as a close second to "shopping portal" for a possible tattoo?) These unicorn offers are for cards that either grant a higher tier status temporarily or, in the case of the American Express Hilton Honors Aspire card, give you top-tier status for as long as you keep the card in your wallet. If you're planning a trip, these can be incredibly valuable.

Like the cards that create pathways to elite status, these cards are used as supporting cast members in my wallet as well.

"Zach, you mentioned status matching. What does that mean?"

It's very simple (phew!). You can take the status you have with an airline, hotel, or car rental company and match it to a competitor or another loyalty program. I'll give you two examples.

As I mentioned, my wife and I have the Amex Hilton Honors Aspire card, which comes with comped Hilton Diamond status. We travel to England a lot, and one of the most convenient car rental companies there is Sixt, as they operate right out of the Sofitel London Heathrow at Terminal 5. One pretty cool thing about Sixt is that they will give you Sixt car rental status if you happen to have hotel elite status. We were able to take our Hilton Diamond status (which we got through our Amex Hilton Honors Aspire card) and match it to Sixt Platinum status. This has saved us hundreds of dollars over the years, since Sixt gives their Platinum members a discount on the base rate.

In early 2022, Delta sent out targeted emails inviting anyone with elite status from another airline to match to Delta. Delta would give you the corresponding status in their program for a set amount of time to try out, and if you wanted to keep it through the next elite year, you'd need to hit certain elite mileage and spending targets during the matched period. This is an example of a combination of status match and status challenge, since there were underlying requirements laid out for keeping the status, as compared to Sixt just giving me the status without the need for any set amount of car rentals.

"Could I take that temporary Delta status and match it to another airline?"

Technically, yes. Most status match opportunities require that you show proof of your airline status and activity in the account. As long as you can fulfill the requirements of the status match, you could pull it off. This is what is commonly referred to as the "Status Match Merry-Go-Round." Once you ascertain one elite status, you can leverage it over and over to keep elite status.

"Zach, I've heard of people booking crazy routing to earn more miles or checking into hotels just to get the elite nights. Is that wise?"

Sometimes you just have to put your butt in a seat or your head on a pillow. Have I booked into a random hotel never to sleep in the bed? Yes. Have I routed myself with multiple connections or flown someplace randomly, all so I could earn more elite miles? You betcha.

These are called mileage runs or mattress runs, and their days are, sadly, coming to an end. In the past, an airline may have required you to fly 100,000 miles in a year to hit top-tier status, and the cheapest tickets earned a point per mile. Nowadays, those same airlines have gutted the miles you earn on the cheapest tickets and instead attach a spending requirement to each elite level. Flying to Tokyo for the day when American Airlines offers $300 round-trip tickets may only earn you 150 elite American Airlines miles rather than the 15,000 miles earned in the past. Years ago, that trip could have been the difference between unlocking eight system-wide upgrades (the ability to upgrade from economy class to business class) and staying mid-tier with no upgrades. Many people would happily spend the day flying to a far-flung location to get that top-tier status and thus the top-tier perks like the guaranteed upgrades.

Don't despair!

Even though loyalty programs are becoming more and more spending based, that doesn't mean there aren't opportunities. There is always opportunity ;). For instance, I'm hoping to keep top-tier Hyatt Globalist status (which requires 60 nights at Hyatt properties) for another year. It is unlikely that I will hit 60 nights organically this year, but I may utilize a mattress run.

A mattress run?

This is where you find cheap hotels that you book to earn the nights but never actually stay in the property. Why would I do this? At 60 nights, Hyatt Globalists get an additional two suite upgrades good for up to 7 nights, plus a free night at any property category 7 and under, and (as long as I have the status) free breakfast. Hyatt prices their category 1 hotels at just 3,500 points per night off-peak. They run promos throughout the year that offer elite members an additional discount, and sometimes they even offer 2X elite night credits.

Let's say I'm 15 nights short, and they run a promo where I get 20 percent off the rate in points. Fifteen nights at 3,500 points a night is 52,500 points less 20 percent, which is 42,000 points. I could either transfer those over from Chase, or Hyatt would probably put them on sale for 1.7 cents to 2 cents apiece. The worst-case scenario would be that it costs me 2 cents per point. Which means I would spend $840 for 15 nights in a hotel, or $56 a night, to qualify for Hyatt Globalist status.

I'd happily spend $840 to get all of those benefits, and it would totally justify me checking into a random category 1 Hyatt for 15 nights and never staying there. This may seem crazy to you, but I'm simply taking the net present value of the impact Globalist status would have on my future travel and saying it's worth far more than the $840 I'd be spending to secure it.

Recap Time

Elite status is only worth something if you extract more value than what it costs to attain it. This could be via butt-in-seat miles or the annual fee on a credit card. For most people, especially those of you looking to take one or two big trips a year, I think you could derive value from elite status gained from a credit card, but many of the other methods may be too much work relative to the benefits gained.

DINING PROGRAMS

Yum.

Did you know that you can link your credit card to your favorite hotel or airline's dining program? Did you even know dining programs existed?

Effectively, after you link your credit card to the dining program, you'll start earning points in the program every time your credit card is used at a participating establishment. Dining programs are one of the easiest ways to earn points in the background of your dining purchases, and they require no work after you link it with your credit card. Pretty tasty.

Note, this is an important thing to keep in mind: Once your credit card is linked to a dining program, it can't be linked to another one.

Here's a list of loyalty programs that have dining programs associated with them:

- Alaska Airlines
- American Airlines
- Delta
- JetBlue
- Spirit
- Southwest

- United
- Hilton
- IHG
- Marriott
- Dosh

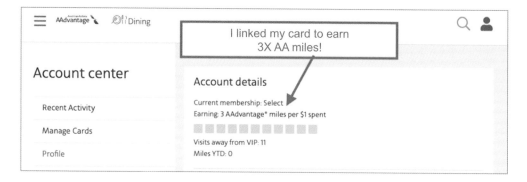

Let's say you have an Amex Gold which earns 4X on dining, and you link that with the American Airlines Aadvantage dining program. Once your card is linked, you can earn 3X American miles whenever you dine at participating restaurants and use your Amex Gold card to pay. You don't even need to do anything; it's just coded into your purchase.

Better yet? Many dining programs have tiers. For instance, the American Airlines dining program has a VIP level that will boost your miles per dollar to 5X if you dine more than 11 times within the program. Now there's a challenge I can get onboard with!

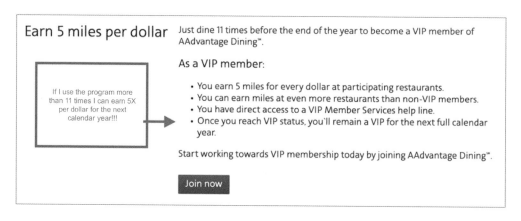

That means every time you dine at participating restaurants you could earn 4X from Amex and up to 5X from American Airlines. That's 9X points.

People ask me all the time how I earn so many points. Well, having the ability to earn multiple kinds of points on purchases certainly helps!

RESELLING ITEMS AND BUYING CLUBS

If you're looking for ways to earn heaps of points and aren't afraid of doing a bit of extra work to earn them, I'd point you toward two separate, but similar, ways to do it:

Reselling items and buying clubs.

Both methods involve you purchasing goods that you have no intention of owning but allow you to earn a lot of points from the purchases, and maybe even a bit of profit. I'll say this on the outset: I've never done either of these, but I know a lot of people who have. Let's break down the basics of how they work and whether it could make sense to you.

Reselling Items

You could approach this like a drop-shipper or being the stock inventory purchaser yourself, but the strategy is much the same. Find a deal on a high demand item, buy a lot of it, and then resell it on Amazon, eBay, or Facebook to earn a lot of points, and maybe even turn a small profit. The way this can be achieved in a time-effective manner is capitalizing on shopping portal bonuses.

Throughout the year, shopping portals will offer major bonuses at big box retailers.

Hypothetically, let's say Dell (a big box retailer) is offering 15X points via Rakuten (a shopping portal). Dell is usually targeted every year around Thanksgiving as part of a big Black Friday promo. Rakuten is set up to allow its members to choose whether they want to earn cash back or American Express points. So your choice would be to get 15 percent off your purchases or earn 15X Amex points on every dollar spent.

So how could we use reselling to earn a lot of points?

One thing many people don't realize is that Dell sells a healthy selection of Bose headphones. Since we know there are good odds of Rakuten offering a 15X deal around Thanksgiving, a few weeks before then, we could take a look at their inventory and see how many headphones they could fulfill. Let's say it's 100 pairs at $300 each, or $30,000 worth of Bose headphones. At 15X, that is 450,000 Amex points. Or we could take the 15 percent off and buy the $30,000 worth of headphones for $25,500, pay with a 2X credit card, and earn 51,000 points from the purchase.

A week before Thanksgiving, we could list the Bose headphones on eBay for $270 apiece (10 percent off) plus shipping (stipulating a ship date after Thanksgiving) and see what the demand of those headphones would be. If all 100 were ordered, we could then buy them on Dell via Rakuten for $25,500 and sell them for $27,000. This would earn us 51,000 points plus $1,500. We'd be responsible for shipping those headphones (hence the work), but we'd earn a tidy profit and 51,000 points.

If we were planning a big trip and wanted the points, we could choose the 15X points instead of the 15 percent cash back and earn over 500,000 points (450,000 plus 51,000) for $3,000 ($30,000 less $27,000). We'd effectively be running a business, so we could sign up for a small business credit card and hit the minimum spending requirement.

Personally, I've never leaned into reselling items with much fervor. But the method is available, and as I said, many people resell items to earn points and miles that they then redeem for aspirational travel.

The primary steps are:

- Buy high-demand items that are easily sold.
- Utilize portal bonuses and credit card category bonuses to earn high-point multiples on purchases.
- Sell the items.
- Net points and/or profit.

Buying Clubs
If reselling items sounds like something you'd be keen on trying out, you may find joining a "buying club" attractive. Buying clubs seek members who are interested in buying items for other members of the club that are of limited quantity, have purchasing restrictions like only one per person, or are hard to find. If you're successful in joining a club, you'll receive notifications regarding products that the group is looking to purchase and need the group's participation in acquiring. Most often these notifications are via a Discord group, private Slack channel, WhatsApp group, or email list.

Buying groups come and go, and there are risks to being a part of them. First of all, you're fronting the capital to purchase the items the group is looking to acquire. Additionally, you'll need to float the money you spend on the items until you are reimbursed by the group. Rarely will you receive payment from a buying group until they have possession of the items you purchased. You'll either have the purchased goods sent directly to the group, or you'll receive them and forward on, but either way this creates a window of time where you're without the product or payment.

Long story short: Be aware of the underlying risks.

A quick Google search will lead you to many buying groups that have been around for quite some time and have garnered trustworthy reputations. One popular item that is often on buying club purchase lists are US Mint coins. These are very collectible, but subject to purchase limits per person. For that reason, many collectors are seeking to buy more than the purchase limitation and seek help from buying groups. Limited run US Mint coins have had the reputation of not only creating an opportunity to earn a lot of points (a set of four coins have eclipsed $5,000 in the past, an easy minimum spending requirement), but often the coins are instantly worth far more than the list price. As a result, many buying clubs will pay you more than the list price, leading to buyers accumulating a bunch of points and profit on the sale. Not bad for a day on the couch pressing "buy" :).

If you decide to pursue a buying club, just make sure you understand the underlying risks and research the buying club you'll be doing business with. Again, add this to the list of methods I've never personally made use of, but know quite a few people who have done so repeatedly with success.

RETENTION OFFERS

Retention offers are sweet, sweet deals that many people have no idea exist. If you're considering canceling a credit card, it is well worth your time to call your bank and inquire if there are any retention offers.

"I like a sweet, sweet deal. How does it work?"

This is an easy one. Turn your card over and call customer service. Let's say it's American Express and you have a Platinum card.

You'd simply call in and say, "Hey there, I'm not really sure I want to keep my card for another year, the annual fee is too high and I'm not making use of the benefits and credits." If you aren't with someone who can handle a retention, you'll be transferred to the retention department.

They will undoubtedly try and convince you to keep the card by explaining the benefits and what you actually took advantage of, so be prepared to answer any questions as to why you wish to cancel. It's worth noting that these conversations are usually on a three-tier system and the representative may earn a bonus if they can convince you to keep the card for another year. From my understanding, that bonus goes down at each tier.

Ordinarily it goes a little something like this:

First offer: They will explain all the amazing benefits of your card, they'll ask you why you want to leave, and they will try and convince you that the card brings more value than whatever reason you gave to leave.

At this stage, you'll have to either say you still want to cancel or you can straight up ask for a retention offer.

Second offer: "Mr. Abel, I totally understand where you're coming from, and we would love to offer you x, y, z to stay." This will either be in the form of points or a statement credit, and usually has a spending requirement associated with it. For example, spend $2,000 in 6 months and get 25,000 points.

Now you don't want to stop there. You want to ask the rep if there are any other offers they could give you.

Third offer: "Mr. Abel, today is your lucky day and this is the *very best we can do*. I can give you 50,000 points if you agree to keep the card another year."

While you won't always get a third offer, it is quite common, and will vary depending on how often you use a card, how much money you spend on it, and how long you've been a customer.

"That does sound sweet, but should I only do this if I want to cancel?"

I think it's worth calling every 2 or 3 years to inquire about any retention offers if you have a card with an annual fee. You won't typically get one every time, but it doesn't hurt to ask. There is one thing I warn against. If you play a game of chicken with cancellation, you may end up getting your card canceled. Meaning, if the representative says there is no better offer, but you think maybe there is another hidden offer that will be revealed if you just insist upon canceling, they may just say, "I'm sorry but that's it" and then process your card cancellation.

Regardless, I think you should always inquire about a retention offer. It never hurts to ask!

DOES IT EVER MAKE SENSE TO PAY FEES TO EARN POINTS?

You may think some of the biggest expenses you make throughout the year are ineligible to earn those sweet, sweet points on. Well, if you're not already seated, sit down, this is quite the doozy.

You may be surprised to learn this, but the money you spend on rent, mortgage, and car payments, even your taxes, can all be paid with a credit card. The catch? Usually, you'll need to pay a processing fee. That begs a question I get every week.

"Does it ever make sense to pay a fee in order to earn points on my purchase?"

The answer is straightforward:

Yes! As long as you're earning points that are more valuable than the fee.

Let's examine the pathway to doing this with the following major purchases:

- Paying your rent with a credit card
- Paying your mortgage or car payment with a credit card
- Paying your taxes with a credit card

How to Pay Rent with a Credit Card

For most of my adult life I have lived in New York City and Los Angeles, two of the most expensive markets in the world for housing. Every month, when rent came due, I felt like I was throwing money into a deep, dark hole. Rent was one of my largest monthly expenses and, aside from a roof over my head, I wasn't getting anything back on my investment. Then, like when the sun blasts through the clouds, I discovered services like RadPad and Plastiq that allow you to charge your rent to them, paying with a credit card, and in return they will mail your landlord a check. I made use of these services multiple times to hit a minimum spending requirement. However, they pass on some pretty hefty fees: usually 2.5 to 3 percent.

Paying a 3 percent processing fee sounds like a lot, and it is, but let's say your rent is $2,500, and you need to hit a minimum spend of $7,500 in 3 months on your American Airlines credit card to earn 100,000 American Airlines miles. If you'd ordinarily spend $5,000 in 3 months, and your rent will put you over the top, that $75 fee is well worth it. As I mentioned, this can be an effective strategy when the points you earn are worth more than the fee you're charged to pay with a credit card.

You could also buy pin-enabled Visa or Mastercard gift cards with a credit card and buy money orders with them, then use the money order to pay your rent. Ordinarily, these gift cards can be purchased at grocery stores or office supply stores, which may earn you a point multiple. Sweet! However, again here comes the charge: there is an activation fee required that is usually $5.95 or $6.95. Something to weigh into your decision on whether you use your credit card for these payments.

This technique of using money orders was much easier 5 to 10 years ago, but now banks look at this unfavorably and could shut your accounts down without rhyme or reason. The main argument they have is that large numbers of money orders can often flag antimoney laundering scrutiny that isn't productive for the bank to deal with, hence they don't mess around and cancel you. For what it's worth, this isn't something I do.

"Zach, is there any way to pay rent with a credit card without a fee?"

Yes. The game changed in 2021 with Bilt Rewards—the first credit card that facilitates fee-free rent payment. Game changer indeed!

My passion for points and entertaining gave me a platform on TikTok, and that platform has opened up a lot of doors, one of which led me to the executive team at Bilt Rewards: a fintech start-up that facilitates renters paying their rent with the Bilt Rewards app fee free. The program took a unique approach to the marketplace by targeting a big hole in point earning: rent.

They partnered with large property management companies all over the country to create an in-app payment portal for a few million apartments. For those who aren't a part of their partner property network, they will send your landlord a check. They even have an ACH payment feature. You simply enter your details in the app, your credit card gets charged, your rent is paid, and you earn points.

"Bish, bash, bosh," as my father-in-law would say.

I wish that Bilt had been around when I was renting, as I would have earned a ton of points every year. My fingers are crossed that they are able to prevail and become one of the major point programs with multiple card offerings.

How to Pay Your Mortgage or Car Payment with a Credit Card

Whether you're a homeowner paying a mortgage, you just leased your first car, or you financed a Range Rover and are taking advantage of IRS Section 179 to fully depreciate your 6,000-pound vehicle, you're making a large payment every month. What if that payment could be used to hit a credit card minimum spending requirement, or could earn you enough points to push you over the threshold to get a fat lie-flat seat to some exotic bucket list location?

Read this way!

Much like you can pay your rent with Plastiq, you can also make a mortgage or car payment via the service as well. The basic strategy stays the same: Only pay a fee if you're earning something more valuable in return. For instance, if you're paying a 3 percent processing fee on a $3,000 mortgage payment and you're not getting more than $90 back in value, don't do it. If you're leveraging a mortgage payment to hit a minimum spend on your credit card to unlock a boatload of points, it could make a lot of sense.

How to Pay Your Taxes with a Credit Card

This is a technique my family has used many times since both of my parents are retired and make quarterly tax payments. Years ago, they just cut a check, but now it's not uncommon for them to eye a new card with a big sign-up bonus that may facilitate future travel. If you're in a similar position, you may utilize this strategy to hit a minimum spending threshold on a card that yields elite miles or an elite dollar waiver on an airline. Paying your taxes with a credit card is super straightforward and it also leaves a distinct paper trail if you should ever be accused of not paying your taxes.

The IRS has a dedicated portal for paying your taxes. I keep an updated page on my site that walks you through the steps, but there is a fee of roughly 2 percent to use a credit card, and a couple bucks if you're using debit.

The IRS currently has three official payment processors that they use to collect payment. Note they all have different processing fees.

First – here's a look at the 3 official payment processors: ACI, Pay1040, payUSAtax.

You'll notice that you can pay your taxes with debit or credit. In fact, Paypal is even possible via PayUsaTax.com .

❯ Debit Card fees $2.20 to $2.55
❯ Credit Card fees up to 1.98%
❯ Digital Wallet Fees – varies

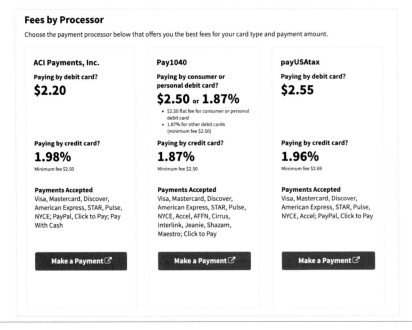

Fees by Processor
Choose the payment processor below that offers you the best fees for your card type and payment amount.

ACI Payments, Inc.	Pay1040	payUSAtax
Paying by debit card?	**Paying by consumer or personal debit card?**	**Paying by debit card?**
$2.20	**$2.50** or **1.87%**	**$2.55**
	• $2.50 flat fee for consumer or personal debit card • 1.87% for other debit cards (minimum fee $2.50)	
Paying by credit card?	**Paying by credit card?**	**Paying by credit card?**
1.98%	**1.87%**	**1.96%**
Minimum fee $2.50	Minimum fee $2.50	Minimum fee $2.69
Payments Accepted Visa, Mastercard, Discover, American Express, STAR, Pulse, NYCE; PayPal, Click to Pay; Pay With Cash	**Payments Accepted** Visa, Mastercard, Discover, American Express, STAR, Pulse, NYCE, Accel, AFFN, Cirrus, Interlink, Jeanie, Shazam, Maestro; Click to Pay	**Payments Accepted** Visa, Mastercard, Discover, American Express, STAR, Pulse, NYCE, Accel; PayPal, Click to Pay
Make a Payment ☑	Make a Payment ☑	Make a Payment ☑

Earn points and pay taxes? It could make sense for a big sign-up bonus. Thanks Uncle Sam!

"Zach, can I do more than one tax payment per year?"

Absolutely. But make sure you pay attention to the number of times you can make payments. Historically, there has been a rule of six. You can make two payments on your annual taxes per payment processor, and two payments per quarter on your estimated quarterly taxes. Since there are three payment processors, you can make six payments per period your taxes are due.

"Why would this be advantageous?"

Let's say you're planning your honeymoon and need a bunch of points. You and your spouse-to-be could sign up for a few cards, use your taxes to hit minimum spending requirements, and the out-of-pocket cost would be the 2 percent processing fee. Not a bad way to make a point haul.

There is also an arbitrage situation that could occur should the right events align. If you look at payments accepted on the payUSAtax site, one of them is PayPal. Often, PayPal is a quarterly 5X/5 percent bonus category on the Chase Freedom Flex credit card. You could pay your taxes and net 3 percent or 3X points. Pretty awesome deal, if you ask me!

Recap
These examples should give you the underlying strategy to adhere to in order to determine whether it's worth it or not to pay a fee to earn points. If you're extracting value in excess of the fee, I say go for it. But remember, everyone values their points differently, and ultimately, it's your discretion and valuation that matters most.

At the end of the day, all of these tips and techniques are offered with the intention of opening your mind to the many ways you can realize your aspirational travel dreams and, if you're a cash-back king, ways you can get a better return on your spending.

HOW TO BEST USE YOUR POINTS AND MILES

When someone asks me to explain how I do what I do, within seconds, I either see a fire light up behind their eyes and I know I've met a kindred spirit, or a glaze quickly forms and I may as well be talking to a wall. If you've made it this far, I'm going to assume there is a fire behind your eyes, and with all the information you have on building credit, tailoring a wallet, and earning points, you're willing to put in the work.

As I began to understand and unlock the incredible possibilities of luxury travel on a budget, I became most obsessed with how to use them on luxury flights and hotels. That's my best use case. Your best use may be offsetting a family trip to Disney, staying in budget hotels in Bali, or doing a 30-day road trip and stretching your points so you can stay free the entire time. "Best use" means something different to each and every person, but achieving it requires understanding your options when it comes time to redeem. This is where most people get lost. It does require a bit of work, but, once you understand it, you're like Neo in *The Matrix* ;).

There are the five big topics I want to focus on when it comes to redemption. If you understand how these five topics work, you'll be able to adjust your strategy as loyalty programs change over time and tailor your wallet in response to them.

1. Transfer partners
2. Airline alliances
3. Award sweet spots
4. Premium cabins
5. Hotels

As I mentioned in the Flexible Points section (page 58) of Your Wallet Needs to Serve Your Goals (page 41), the following programs all have transfer partners or the ability to convert bank points into a partner program's award currency.

- American Express Membership Rewards
- Bilt Rewards
- Brex
- Capital One Miles
- Chase Ultimate Rewards
- Citi ThankYou Rewards
- Marriott Bonvoy Points

"Thanks for the list, Zach, but how do you know when to transfer an' when to use the portal?"

Rule of Thumb #1: Only transfer if you can beat the portal.

Understanding where to look, and why, is integral to maximizing the value of your points, as well as extending the longevity of your points. In 2021, Chase had an incredible 100,000-point offer on the Chase Sapphire Preferred. It required spending $4,000 in 3 months, so if you hit that spend right on the nose, you'd be sitting on 104,000 Chase Ultimate Rewards. You could use those for $1,250 in the Chase travel portal, or you could take advantage of their transfer partners.

The partners on the next page, as of June 2022, were all 1:1 transfer partners of Chase. This means you could take those 104,000 Chase points and convert them into 104,000 points of any of the programs listed on the next page.

Did we mention we like Chase Ultimate Rewards?

If you're going to transfer your Chase points, you need to get more value out of your transferred 104,000 points than you'd get in the Chase portal, or $1,300. Always, always, always check to see if any of the partners are pricing the flights you want cheaper than the portal you're switching from (in this case, the Chase travel portal).

In this example, we're featuring a Chase Sapphire Preferred card, but the concept applies across the board. You want to make sure that using a transfer partner creates more value per point than you could get just using the portal. This is one of the main reasons I almost never transfer to IHG or Marriott. IHG will sell their points for 0.5 cent apiece and Marriott will dip as low as 0.8 cent apiece. Why on earth would I trade points worth a minimum of 1.25 cents apiece for something I could buy for much, much less? There are exceptions to any rule, like for an overwater villa in the Maldives, when you've hit your purchased point limit and need more points for redemption. But I adhere to that basic rule of thumb.

Rule of Thumb #2: Make sure there is award availability before transferring points.

Let's say you want to go to the Maldives and stay at the Park Hyatt. You look and see that it's $1,000 a night in the Chase travel portal, so you'd need 80,000 points per night if booking in the portal (1.25 cents per point). You've also been reading my blog (give yourself some extra credit!) and know that the Park Hyatt Maldives is 30,000 World of Hyatt points per night.

So you transfer to Hyatt to book, right? Not yet.

We like to stay under the radar when we fly first class ;) Japan Airlines 2019 from LAX to Tokyo with a final destination of Singapore.

If you wanted to transfer to Hyatt instead of using the portal, The Park Hyatt Maldives would need to have base room availability. If they did, you'd transfer Chase to Hyatt and stay for 30,000 points per night. That's nearly 3 nights for the price of 1 in the portal. But they may not have the award space available, and if you already transferred your points without checking availability, your precious points would be stuck. Aside from unique situations, point transfers are distinctly one way. You can't undo a bank-to-partner transfer. Da da daaaaaaaaa. (Too dramatic? I told you I was an actor, right?)

Rule of Thumb #3: Not all transfer partners offer equal value.

The more you look at redemption rates (which means a lot, if you're me), the better you'll get at formulating a valuation for each partner's points as a baseline. (It's basically my love language at this point.) You will learn which programs consistently offer fantastic value and which do not. For instance, I tend to think if you can get a penny a point on IHG, Hilton, or Marriott points, you're doing a darn good job. I won't say never, but seldom do I transfer Chase or Amex to any of those programs. On the flip side, if you're transferring points to airlines to fly in premium cabins, you may consistently get 2 cents, 3 cents, 4 cents, or even 10 cents per point if you really hit a home run. I've been fortunate to fly Japan Airlines first class a few times between the US and Japan for 80,000 American miles. This flight can often cost $10,000-plus retail. *Ten thousand dollars*! (Matching tees not included in ticket price.)

Now we'll apply Rules #1 and #2 to a mock trip.

Let's say you have 500,000 Chase Ultimate Rewards and you want to go to the Maldives.

Rule #1, beat the portal.

You've researched hotels and you love both the Park Hyatt and the Intercontinental. They're each pricing around $1,000 in the Chase portal, or 80,000 Ultimate Rewards per night, and that's the number to beat.

Rule #2, make sure the partner has availability.

- You check Hyatt and find that Park Hyatt is pricing villas at 30,000 per night.
  - » So, yes, pricing is lower than the portal.
- You check IHG and find that Intercontinental is pricing them at 120,000 IHG points.
  - » Their pricing is higher than the portal.

For the Park Hyatt, you would transfer your Chase Ultimate Reward points to Hyatt points. For the Intercontinental, you would use the Chase travel portal.

Staying at the Intercontinental would mean you could book 6 nights in the portal, or 6 times 80,000 a night equals 480,000. Whereas, if you chose the Park Hyatt Maldives, you could stay 16 nights at 30,000 a night, or you could stay 6 nights and have 320,000 Ultimate Rewards left over for flights.

Speaking of flights.

It just so happens that you can transfer Chase Ultimate Rewards to British Airways Avios. Avios is the currency of British Airways, Iberia, Aer Lingus, and Qatar Airways. If you transfer into any of those programs, you can move it between airlines. Each of those airlines keep different award charts for redemption on their planes and their partners. My website, MonkeyMiles.com, has a chart with all the current transfer partners for airlines and hotels.

The goal would be to see if we could move Chase Ultimate Rewards into that program. I've been doing this a long time and know that Qatar Airways prices business-class flights from the US to the Maldives via Doha at just 85,000 each way. Qatar Airways isn't a partner of Chase's, but do you know who is? British Airways.

We would apply the same strategy. Check the portal for pricing. Then we would look and see if Qatar Airways has award space available at 85,000 each way, or 170,000 round trip. If the 170,000 round trip was cheaper than the Chase portal, we would move points to British Airways, link our account to Qatar Airways, and book the world's best business class (Qsuites) for 85,000 miles each way from the US to the Maldives via Doha.

I've been lucky enough to fly Qsuites on a number of occasions and it completely spoils you. Like, a private chef, a $100 bottle of champagne, and four people creating quad seating spoils you.

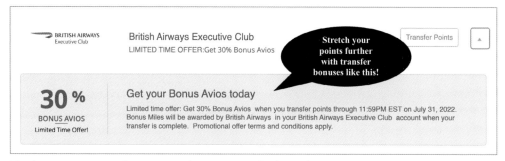

The best time to transfer points is during a transfer bonus!

My parents, Dave, and I all flew back from the Middle East in Qatar Airways famed QSuites. The 4 lie-flat seats all combined into one quad where we could dine and chat together.

Rule of Thumb #3: Always be aware of transfer bonuses.

Let's say that the situation works out and you can book via Qatar Airways for 170,000 points per person round trip, or 340,000 total points. You'd be just a tad bit short, and you could either use points to stay 5 nights in the Maldives, and either buy Hyatt points or use cash for the 6th night, or strategically transfer your points to British Airways when there is a transfer bonus.

"Wait, wait, wait, you're just gonna skip over the part where you transferred to BA then to Qatar? Very confusing, totally lost, please explain."

I was wondering if you were going to say anything about that :).

If you're looking to consistently get the highest rate of return on your points, you'll need to understand how "Airline Alliances" open the door to award sweet spots in premium cabins. If you're flying more than 7 hours, flying in business and first class transforms your entire trip. You get expedited check-in, security, lounge access, and, the best part of all, a bed to sleep in so you arrive rested and ready to explore your destination. Premium cabins are where I spend the most points, and ultimately the focal point of how I build trips.

Rule of Thumb #4: Look for airline alliances, award sweet spots, and premium cabins.

Airlines can have singular partnerships with other airlines, and they can also be members of a large group of airlines called an alliance. There are currently three big airline alliances in the world: Star Alliance, oneworld, and SkyTeam.

Star Alliance	oneworld	SkyTeam
Aegean Airlines	Alaska Airlines	Aeroflot
Air Canada	American Airlines	Aerolíneas Argentinas
Air China	British Airways	Aeromexico
Air India	Cathay Pacific	AirEuropa
Air New Zealand	Finnair	Air France
All Nippon Airways	Iberia	China Airlines
Asiana	Japan Airlines	China Eastern
Austrian Airlines	Malaysia Airlines	Czech Airlines
Avianca	Qantas	Delta
Brussels Airlines	Qatar	Garuda Indonesia
Copa Airlines	Royal Air Maroc	Kenya Airways
Croatia Airlines	Royal Jordanian	KLM
EgyptAir	S7 Airlines	Korean Air
Ethiopian Airlines	SriLankan	MEA
EVA Air		Saudia
LOT Polish Airlines		Tarom
Lufthansa		Vietnam Airlines
Scandinavian Airlines		XiamenAir
Shenzhen Airlines		
Singapore Airlines		
South African Airways		
Swiss Airlines		
TAP Portugal		
Thai Airways		
Turkish Airlines		
United Airlines		

Here is an example of how American is partnered individually with another airline, but is also in an alliance:

- American is partnered with JetBlue. JetBlue isn't a part of any alliance.
- American is also a part of the oneworld alliance, which means it's partnered with all of the other member airlines.

How to Best Use Your Points and Miles

I've had the great fortune of visiting the Japan Airlines lounge on numerous occasions, and the all-you-can-eat sushi bar is my favorite perk. I practically licked the counter clean.

Whether you're a singular partner or part of an airline alliance, airlines usually have one award redemption rate for their own flights, and then a separate redemption rate for their partner's flights. For instance, if you wanted to fly from the US to London, American Airlines has rates specifically for American Airlines operated flights, and then they also have rates if you were to fly on a partner, like British Airways or JetBlue. Those rates may even be different depending on the partner. These partnerships may also permit the extension of certain benefits associated with carrying elite status, like upgrades, free checked bags, lounge access, and even the ability to earn bonus points on cash flights.

Here's an example. We now know that oneworld is one of the three airline alliances. If you carry oneworld Emerald status, which is their top-tier status, it grants you first-class lounge access when flying internationally, regardless of your booking cabin. If you were to fly in Japan Airlines business class, but have oneworld Emerald status via American Airlines, you could still enter the first-class lounge when flying business class. This is because American Airlines and Japan Airlines are both in the oneworld alliance.

To be a travel hacking whiz when it comes to using points, we want to home in on booking partner flights—specifically, the ability to find cheaper redemptions using these alliances and partnerships.

You guessed it, I'm coming in hot with an example for you.

For instance, if you see saver award availability to fly Air France business class from New York to Paris, and you carry an American Express card, you have a few transfer options. The most obvious would be to transfer to Air France's Flying Blue loyalty program. But before you pull the trigger, you need to check to see if there are other ways you could book that same ticket.

Amex has some of the best transfer partners in the biz.

OK travel sleuths, here's what we know:

- Air France is a member of SkyTeam, so SkyTeam partners may have access to those award tickets.
- Air France also maintains individual partnerships that we need to check as well.

Who are the Air France partners you have access to via American Express?

If we look at the Amex transfer partners above and cross-reference them with SkyTeam (page 131) we see: Aeromexico and Delta. In addition to being a member of SkyTeam, Air France also has individual partners. Virgin Atlantic is listed as one and it's also an Amex transfer partner. We may be able to book our Air France business-class flight from any of these programs.

"Zach. With me being a travel detective now, I notice you're saying 'may be able to book.' Why?"

Airlines have different tiers of award space that they release. The lowest category is often referred to as saver space. This is the award space that partners can book with their miles. In the past, airlines were more transparent with how they decide what is saver space and what isn't. These days, many airlines are using variable or dynamic pricing, and it's quite difficult to determine when partners will have access and when they won't.

In this example, let's say Air France is pricing flights at 57,500 miles plus $200. In August, they may consider this saver space, and partner airlines could book with their own currency. In December, more off-season, they may not consider the 57,500 miles saver space, and instead, 55,000 miles is saver space. Do you think these airlines are doing it on purpose to make it harder to redeem miles? Me too.

Which transfer partner do you choose?

This is where it becomes subjective. It's a combination of how many points are required to book from each program, the taxes and surcharges each program levies, and how you value a partner's mileage program.

Let's say Air France wants 57,500 miles plus $200 for our New York to Paris flight in January 2023.

And we know we can book with the following partners:

Delta

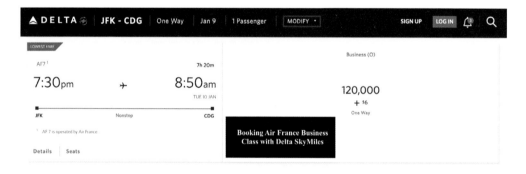

Virgin Atlantic

Aeromexico

Hopefully a side-by-side comparison helps you realize the vast array of award pricing tied to the same flight. I think this is a no-brainer. I'd transfer to Virgin Atlantic, which is 9,000 points cheaper than Air France/KLM Flying Blue, but $72 more expensive. Unquestionably, I value 9,000 Amex points way more than $72.

What are some common award sweet spots?

This is an ever-evolving list, but here are my current top ten.

(Disclaimer: They are all international business-class and first-class flights. There are many domestic economy redemptions that I haven't included. The main reason is that starting in early 2022, it's been increasingly difficult to redeem foreign carrier miles on Delta, United, American, or Alaska Airlines within the US. In the past, you could redeem the miles of Avianca, British Airways, Singapore, and Turkish quite competitively in the US, including to Hawaii. The trend is that the US-based carriers are restricting this award space to partners, and I don't see this changing any time soon.)

With that, here are my Top 10 Award Sweet Spots. (All of these are insane ways to fly, so proceed with caution. Remember, once you fly flat, you never go back.)

1. US to Europe or Europe to Dubai in Emirates First Class

- New York/JFK to Milan for 85,000 miles

- Newark to Athens for 85,000 miles

- Most European cities to Dubai for 85,000 miles

2. ANA Round Trip Business Class

- US to Europe for 88,000 miles

    » Reduced surcharges booking on Air Canada, LOT, Scandinavian Airlines, Turkish Airlines, or United

- US to Asia for 75,000 miles

    » Reduced surcharges on ANA, Asiana Airlines, Air China, Air New Zealand, or Etihad

When my wife and I arrived in Dubai after this first class Emirates flight, an Emirates employee was waiting to escort us to a golf cart that then drove us straight to the first class lounge. Absolutely insane.

Flying Delta One from London to Atlanta for just 38k Chase points.

We booked 3 Singapore Suites from Beijing to Singapore as part of my mom's surprise 75th birthday trip around the world.

3. Virgin Atlantic to Fly ANA from US to Japan
- First class
  » West Coast to Japan for 55,000 miles
  » East Coast to Japan for 60,000 miles
- Business class
  » West Coast to Japan for 45,000 miles
  » East Coast to Japan for 47,500 miles

4. Delta One Suites with Virgin Atlantic Miles to Fly ANA from US to Japan
- US to Europe for 50,000 miles

5. Singapore Suites
- US to Frankfurt for 97,000 miles

6. Alaska Airlines to Fly Cathay Pacific
- First class
  » US to Asia for 70,000 miles
  » Australia via Hong Kong to US for 80,000 miles
- Business class
  » US to Asia for 55,000 miles
  » US to Australia for 55,000 miles

Dave took this picture in Cathay First Class before we flew 15 hours from Hong Kong to Chicago in the winter of 2017. We stayed up for hours drinking $200 scotch and ended up just sleeping a couple of hours. So much fun and 70k Alaska Miles.

After my wife wrapped her TV show, we flew around the world. Our final leg was on Lufthansa First Class on the A380 to LA, which we booked for just 87k Avianca Lifemiles a piece.

7. Alaska Airlines to Fly Qantas
   - First class
     » US to Australia for 70,000 miles
   - Business class
     » US to Australia for 55,000 miles

8. Qatar Airways Qsuites with American Airlines Miles
   - US to Middle East and India for 70,000 miles
   - US to Africa for 75,000 miles

9. Turkish Airlines Business Class
   - US to Europe for 45,000 miles
   - US to Far East Asia for 67,500 miles
   - US to South Africa for 85,000 miles

10. Avianca to Europe and Asia
   - Europe
     » First class for 87,000 miles
     » Business class for 63,000 miles
   - Asia
     » First class for 90,000 miles
     » Business class for 75,000 miles

READY FOR A RECAP?

I almost always utilize transfer partners, which is why I keep soooooo many credit cards. I want to have access to as many transfer partners as possible and be able to get as many bonus points per dollar on my spending as possible. When it comes time to redeem, I know I'll be able to assure the best possible deal.

OK, the recap:

- Check pricing in the portal.
- Check pricing with transfer partners to beat the portal.
- Utilize airline partnerships and alliances:
    » Compare options.
    » Research the latest sweet spots.
    » Take advantage of any transfer bonuses.
- Book the cheapest and most high-value redemption.

Perhaps the most important step: Check out MonkeyMiles.com for news on sweet spots and transfer bonuses. And, well, more me ;).

YOU MAY BE A SMALL BUSINESS AND NOT EVEN KNOW IT

Game. Changer.

When I learned that you don't need an EIN (employer identification number) to open small business credit cards, the sky parted, rays of sunlight poured onto my wallet, and I knew I had cracked another egg to feed the insatiable point monster within.

I know what you're thinking, *Zach, this sounds like you're gaming the system.*

Au contraire mon frère. (I learned this on my Air France flight from Atlanta to Paris on their new A350.) What I'm doing is making the system work for *you.*

Let's break it down into four topics that bend the system to your will. (Remember, you are Neo now.)

- The gig economy has changed everything.
- Make tax season a little easier with segregated expenses.
- Improve your personal credit score.
- Have multiple versions of the same card.

The gig economy made a lot of people de facto small business owners.

Whether you're firing up Uber during a surge to collect some side cash, finding employment on Upwork or Fiverr, or simply dog walking to subsidize your ambitions as a Broadway superstar, the gig economy is impacting many of us all now. My guess is, on any given day, we all encounter someone who is receiving payment via the gig economy aside from their W2 income.

What does this mean?

It means if you have a side hustle, work the gig economy full time, or maybe are starting an online book company in your parent's garage that will one day send you to space in a gigantic phallic rocket and haven't incorporated yet, you're probably an independent contractor and receive a 1099 to file with our friends at the IRS.

"Yes, Zach, I do. Why should I care?"

I'm no accountant, but if you're not receiving W2 income and you are paying expenses integral to your work, you're what I consider a de facto small business.

"Zach, how is that possible?"

A lot of businesses that ultimately end up incorporating, or filing DBAs (doing business as), start out as sole proprietorships or individuals working as independent contractors. GaryVee famously documents his weekend garage sale victories: He buys things on the cheap, and then sells them for outrageous gains on eBay. He's worth nine figures, and does it as a hobby, but there are many people just like him who subsidize their income with a side hustle. These side hustles require investment and expenses, expenses that should be itemized and potentially deducted come tax time.

Credit card companies pave the way for you to apply for small business credit cards via a sole proprietorship. How? You can apply using your Social Security number in lieu of an EIN. You fill out all the information truthfully as it applies to your side hustle and your personal income.

Let me give you an example; we all know by now that I love an example (or *exemple* if I'm speaking French again).

Let's say you're a grad student and a math whiz. You're tutoring kids on the side, and they pay you via PayPal. You'll receive a 1099 at the end of the year on that income. But what if you're driving your car to their location, paying for parking and gas, hosting a website, designing an online course to scale your tutoring talents, and advertising your bad mamma jamma course on Facebook?

Again, I'm no accountant and you should certainly seek the advice of a professional, but those sound like expenses to me. And those expenses should be itemized and accounted for so they can be deducted.

What better way to do this than to have a separate credit card for those expenses?

You could apply for a small business credit card with your Social Security number and personal income and use it for the expenses of your burgeoning tutoring empire. Suddenly all of these incredible credit card offers that you see for small business credit cards are available to you. I've earned millions of points with small business credit cards via sign-up bonuses, bonus categories, referral bonuses, and retention offers.

Small business credit cards are a great way to accumulate points on an ongoing basis, itemize your expenses, and minimize the effect it has on your personal credit.

"What do you mean by minimize the effect on my personal credit?"

I'm so happy you asked :), and it has been a while since we've covered this.

When you apply for a small business credit card, your personal credit profile is pulled, so you'll get a temporary ding to your score. Usually, it's a handful of points and bounces back within a month or two. While the inquiry will have a small impact on your score, the true value is found in moving those business purchases off your personal cards and away from your personal credit report.

Here's the sauce.

A lot of banks don't report the purchases you're making on small business credit cards to your personal credit report. Currently, and this changes all the time, the only banks that report those expenses are Discover, Capital One, and Wells Fargo.

Why does this matter?

In the very first chapter of this book, you'll recall the five factors of your credit score. One of the very biggest is utilization. Remember, utilization is the amount of your total credit that you use divided by the total amount of credit available to you. It makes up nearly a third of your entire credit score, and keeping it under 10 percent is the goal. If your credit card company doesn't report your business spending activity to personal credit bureaus, it will aid you in keeping that number lower.

So not only are you earning mega points and itemizing your expenses to make it easier come tax time, you're also improving your personal credit score without much effort at all. Win-win!

Let me tell you how I've put this into practice.

Depending on the month, I hold somewhere between 15 and 25 credit cards. Now roughly half of those are business credit cards. I even hold multiples of the same card. I know, I'm kind of extreme. This means that all of the expenses that end up on those cards aren't reported to my personal credit report and aid me in keeping my utilization number under 10 percent.

"Hollllld up. You said you have multiples of the same card?"

Yep. While many banks won't let you hold more than one version of a personal credit card (although there are exceptions and back doors), many banks will issue you multiple versions of the same business credit card to service each business entity you own. Lemme give you a little background.

My first business was . . . me!

I'm an actor, and one of the things you do once you hit an income threshold as an actor is incorporate. Actors pay a commission to their agents and managers, and we only receive a fraction of the salary we're paid on a project. To be able to deduct this commission from our taxes, we need to incorporate. Once you're earning enough money, the fees associated with keeping and maintaining a business (or corporation) are offset by the savings in tax deductions (as you only pay tax on your income after you have deducted your expenses, which is known as your net income). When you incorporate, the government gives your business an employer identification number, or an EIN.

The funny thing is, my accountant never even told me about small business credit cards, or that I could apply for one using my EIN, let alone as a sole proprietor.

I started off just allocating one personal card solely for business expenses. While this isn't wrong, it wasn't optimal to me at the time, or now. Actually, that's not funny at all. Think of the points I lost out on! Someone get me a bag to breathe into!

Thankfully, that all changed once I became obsessed with points and the credit card ecosystem.

The first thing that I did was open credit cards specifically for my EIN, but you could do the same thing as a sole proprietor. Not only did my point balances skyrocket, but my credit score also improved because thousands of dollars suddenly weren't being put on a personal credit card and reported to the credit bureaus.

As mentioned earlier, in 2014 I had back surgery that didn't really clear up any of the pain I was experiencing. In fact, it made things worse and sidelined my acting career. While I was trying to figure out what I was going to do, I created MonkeyMiles.com.

It was a complete side gig. A passion hobby that I thought, who knows, maybe it'll take off, maybe it won't, but I'm going to structure it as a business either way.

My first business credit card associated with Monkey Miles was opened as a sole proprietorship. If you're unsure how you want to organize your business, you can just start it as a sole proprietorship, and apply for credit cards with your Social Security number. Any expenses I accrued as a result of investing in the development of the blog, I did my best to put on those credit cards.

Here's the best part.

Many banks don't have restrictions on a business owner getting the same card for each business they own. This is certainly not a universal rule, and make sure you do your due diligence. But I found myself getting sign-up bonuses for Monkey Miles on cards that I already had in my wallet that were opened with my EIN. My EIN could have one card and my sole proprietorship (using my Social Security number) could have another.

As the popularity of Monkey Miles grew, I splintered off an awards consulting business. People would hire me to make the best use of their points. I viewed this as a completely different business from the blog and took it as an opportunity to open more credit cards to itemize those expenses. With the popularity of TikTok, I now generate income from social media too and have created another business. Each time, I open credit cards for that particular business's expenses.

One thing to keep in mind, if you're operating as a sole proprietorship, you'll need to pay attention to rules that restrict sign-up bonuses, welcome offers, etc. For instance, if I were to get a Chase Ink Business Preferred card for Monkey Miles and then wanted to get another one for my awards booking business, I'd need to wait 24 months after receiving the bonus to apply. However, if you have separate EINs, you may not be restricted by the same rule.

"Zach, could you give me examples of who may qualify?"

- Tutors
- Uber and Lyft drivers (assuming they still get 1099s whenever you're reading this)
- DoorDash, Grubhub, and Postmates employees
- Bloggers
- People who make money on social media (TikTok, Instagram, YouTube)
- Catering waiters
- Personal trainers
- Babysitters
- Dog walkers
- Consultants
- Freelance graphic designers and web designers
- Singers, artists, dancers, models, and magicians
- Virtual assistants
- EBay, Amazon, and Facebook resellers

The list goes on and on. As long as you open the business as a sole proprietor and are collecting a 1099, you can open a business credit card.

"This seems great, but how do you manage the annual fees?"

It's like you're reading my mind, as well as my book ;).

I will be the first to admit that I am at the far end of the spectrum when it comes to the number of credit cards I keep in my "wallets," the fees I'm willing to pay, and the level of accounting I'm willing to do to keep everything straight. But it doesn't have to be expensive or complicated to reap serious benefits.

Let's use Chase as an example. You know I love an example.

Chase has built a wonderful ecosystem with their point system, Chase Ultimate Rewards. They have two different kinds of Ultimate Rewards. The regular kind can only be used in their portal, for cash back/statement credit, but they can't be transferred into partner programs. Chase also has cards that earn premium Ultimate Rewards that can be used in the portal or transferred into partner programs.

As long as you have one of their premium Ultimate Rewards credit cards, you can move regular Ultimate Rewards into that account and instantly they become transferable. This goes for business and personal cards.

As an example, Chase offers no-annual-fee personal credit cards that have bonus categories, have unlimited 1.5X earning, and, aside from keeping your expenses segregated, add no additional cost to your bottom line. If your business kept a Chase Ink Business Preferred as the lead role of your credit card portfolio (aka your premium card), any points that you earn via those personal cards could be merged with your premium card (in this case the Chase Ink Business Preferred card) and transferred to partner programs.

You could optimize your spending categories, segregate expenses, and earn a load of points, all for $95 a year in fees (the annual fee on the Chase Ink Business Preferred). Not too shabby.

I use business and personal credit cards in tandem, and while I have multiple EINs, I also continue to start things out as a sole proprietorship. As I said before, I have earned millions of points using a combination of small business credit cards and personal credit cards to optimize every dollar I spend. Make sure you do the due diligence of assessing the fees, consulting with your financial adviser, and comparing benefits, but it's a piece of my strategy that has been extremely rewarding to me.

You May be a Small Business and Not Even Know It

TRAVEL HACKING WITHOUT USING CREDIT CARDS

While credit cards help A LOT when it comes to getting a great deal, you don't have to have them to make it all happen. There are a few tricks of the trade that will certainly help you hack a trip and stretch your buck. These are the areas we will concentrate on:

- Google Flights plus ITA Matrix
- Using a VPN to save you money
- Positioning flights
- One-way flights vs. round trip
- Hidden city ticketing
- Checking account bonuses and/or earn points plus miles on deposits
- VIP hotel programs

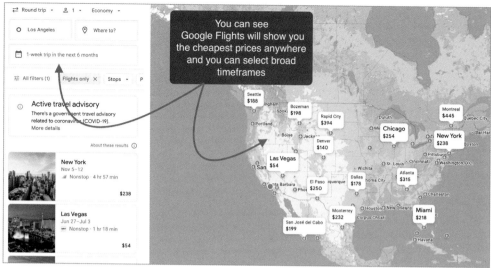

If you're flexible...deals are everywhere.

GOOGLE FLIGHTS PLUS ITA MATRIX

I'm always amazed by the number of people who have no idea about Google Flights. It's a wonderful search tool powered by ITA. ITA is an algorithm that scours the Internet and gives you the ability to set alerts, search on a map for the cheapest flights, and will even email you when prices change. And it's completely freeeee.

We can use a trip out of Los Angeles as an example. If you leave "where to" blank and click the map, it'll tell you where you can fly cheapest. You can select which month you'd like to travel, whether you'd like a weekend trip, and if you'd like to leave in 1 or 2 weeks, and it even allows you to search up to 6 months at a time.

If you want to go next level on your searching, including specifying exact routing, fare buckets, connection times, and some deep geek level travel wizardry, go to the ITA Matrix—also owned by Google. This tool was developed by MIT scientists (in my mind, they wear white coats and have clipboards—regardless, they're smarty-pants) and is the most powerful search tool in the business. It's also the most complex and comprehensive around. Honestly, an entire book could be written just on using the ITA Matrix. If it's something you're interested in pursuing, there are many guides and tutorials out there to get as geeky and complex as your heart desires. I cannot guarantee they will corroborate the clipboard/white coat combo, but lemme know what you find out.

One thing to note, ITA Matrix doesn't facilitate booking. However, someone created a site called bookwithmatrix.com; you simply copy and paste your ITA Matrix search results into their search bar, and it will show you where you can buy it.

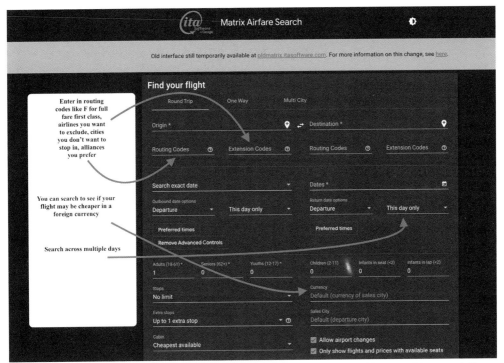

If you want to go down the rabbit hole of fare construction...the ITA Matrix will be your bff.

USING A VPN MAY SAVE YOU MONEY

A VPN (virtual private network) allows you to route your Internet activity through a different server that could be in a foreign country. This can be advantageous because travel consolidators, as well as airlines, hotels, and car rental agencies, often price their products and services differently depending on where they think the demand may be highest.

Let's say you want to fly from the US to Germany for Oktoberfest. (Yes, I use this example because what could be better than typing "Oktoberfest." I hope you're using the correct accent.) It may be worth your time to fire up the ole VPN and place yourself in Ireland or Thailand or New Zealand. Why? There are a lot more people searching for flights from the US to Germany in the US than there would be in Ireland, Thailand, or New Zealand.

I did a quick search and found that flights were $28 cheaper to fly Lufthansa economy from New York to Frankfurt if you placed yourself in Ireland rather than in the US. The next round of beer and Brezens is on you!

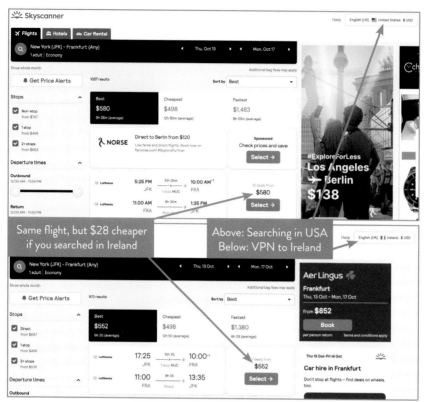

Every dollar counts! It's amazing how often a VPN can save you some extra cash.

POSITIONING FLIGHTS

I have done this so many times and cumulatively have saved loads of money. Instead of departing from a big hub or your nearest small airport, take a quick flight, drive, or train to a different city where the pricing is much more advantageous. Elizabeth and I have done this for years going to and from England. Flying out of London is egregiously expensive. However, if you're willing to fly out of Paris, Stockholm, Inverness, or Dublin, the prices can be muuuuch cheaper and the long-haul portion of your flight may be the same.

Let's say you wanted to fly on the 4 p.m. British Airways flight from London to LA, but you found it's cheaper to fly out of Dublin to start your journey. The best way to do it would be to buy a cheap flight to Dublin the night before (although I've chanced it many times and flown in the same day). In Dublin, you'd hop on the plane that would then fly back to London. After a short layover, you'd be on the 4 p.m. British Airways flight you originally had your eye on to Los Angeles.

There was a string of months where business-class flights out of Dublin to LA were consistently $1,500 to $2,000 round trip with a connection in London. The same flight out of London to LA was $5,000-plus in business class and $1,200 to $1,500 in economy class. Crazy to think that by just buying a $100 flight to Dublin and starting there meant I was paying nearly the same to fly in business class as many were paying to fly in economy.

Of course, it took more time to fly to Dublin and back, but I was also earning a ton of miles. There was a period of about 2 years when Alaska Airlines was giving so many miles to British Airways flights that every round-trip business-class ticket I booked to or from Europe was earning me enough points to fly back one way in business class. As the Irish would say, "Not a bad craic!" (I cannot guarantee they would say that, but please do read it with the accent.)

ONE-WAY FLIGHTS VS. ROUND TRIP

You should always look at both one-way and round-trip options. I have found flights that are cheaper when booked round trip than one way, and I've found splitting a round trip up and booking it as two single flights to be cheaper. It's also worth looking at mixing and matching airlines. I do this all the time with award bookings, but it's also a good practice to incorporate in your deal search when investigating cash fares.

HIDDEN CITY TICKETING

This is what's known as skiplagging. It sounds like a Shakespearean swear word, and while you could utilize it as such, in the travel world it refers to the practice of buying a multiconnection ticket with the intention of only flying one of the legs and throwing away the rest. In other words, you want to fly A to B, but the airline is pricing A to B to C cheaper, so you buy the flight with a layover in the city you actually want to fly into, and throw the B to C leg away.

Let's revisit our earlier example where we were flying business class to Los Angeles from London but popped over to Dublin to start the journey and then routed back via London (making it much cheaper). The problem with doing this is that the return is also going to take you back to Dublin. Your outbound ticket would be Dublin to London to LA, and the return would be LA to London to Dublin. And then you would collect your bags in Dublin, go through immigration, and fly back again to London on a separate ticket. The ticket price is cheaper, but it's also adding two more flights when you have already landed in the city that is your desired final destination.

But what if you didn't take that last leg and just got off the plane in London? If you have bags, they will go on to Dublin. If you don't have bags, and you walk off the plane and into London, you just skiplagged. You bloody skiplagger! Airlines are *not* fans of this behavior, and the biggest warning I could give you is to not do it very often. People have been banned, have had their elite status and mileage revoked, and have even been tried in court cases where the airline sued them for the money they say should have been paid. So proceed with caution.

Travel Hacking Without Using Credit Cards

This kind of thing works on award flights too. For instance, if you want to fly from London to New York or Atlanta, Delta will usually charge you a ton of points. However, if you book to Mexico City, suddenly you may see options where the price plummets and still routes through Atlanta or New York just like you wanted. I've seen prices go from 300,000-plus points to just 65,000. But as I mentioned, this isn't something I advise doing or advocate. I'm just simply alerting you to something that can be done.

If this is something you're intrigued by, I'd suggest checking out the website skiplagged.com.

CHECKING ACCOUNT BONUSES AND/OR EARNING POINTS PLUS MILES ON DEPOSITS

There is a lot of money to be made simply by opening checking accounts when they're offering a bonus tied to a new deposit. You can keep your money there for a little while, and then when you see another bank offer a great deal, move your money, get the bonus, and just keep rinsing and repeating.

Personally, I've never done this because of the bookkeeping involved. A lot of people partake in this and can make thousands per year, simply by shifting money here and there to take advantage of deposit bonuses.

Another option that has enticed me lately, and one I may take advantage of, is the company Bask Bank. When it comes to opening a bank account with them, they give you an option: Earn interest or earn American Airline miles. That's right, you could earn airline miles on your money that's just sitting there! They offer 1 mile for every dollar you have deposited with them annually. The miles are based on your average balance over the course of 12 months. If you have $10,000 on average, you'll earn 10,000 miles. If you have $500,000 on average, you'll earn 500,000 miles. Nice easy math.

People who would opt to put their money into an account like this and not into an investment opportunity would likely go for the cash back rather than the American Airlines miles as a bonus for their savings account. I totally understand this. But if we look closer (you know how I love to look closerrrrr), it does become more interesting.

Often people like to have at least 6 months' worth of expenses in cash in their bank account. The choice is either to earn a low interest rate on your money that's sitting there or some sweet American miles. At the time of writing this book, the APY (annual percentage yield) your money will earn sitting in a savings account is 1.5 percent. Let's say you had $70,000 in cash in your Bask Bank account. That would mean you'd earn $1,050 instead of 70,000 American Airlines miles. Currently, 70,000 American Airlines miles would get you a Qsuite business-class flight to the Maldives, which is worth way more than $1,050.

It's always worth thinking about how the potential earnings from your hard-earned cash can work best for you! Keep up to date with the latest offerings from companies like Bask Bank at MonkeyMiles.com!

VIP HOTEL PROGRAMS

What if I told you that hotels have secret VIP booking programs that *anyone can use* and that offer the *same rate as the best available rate*. Finding out about these sneaky, secret deals makes me *so excited.* I'm always amazed at how many people are completely unaware that such programs exist. Here's how it works.

We flew to Beijing for a weekend while my wife was filming her show. When the hotel learned we both worked in the entertainment industry, the dessert chef constructed a dark chocolate camera featuring the Union Jack and American flag. We posed for this picture in our upgraded suite courtesy of booking via Pen Club...their VIP program that anyone can use.

In order to make use of these VIP programs you need to work with an adviser of the program. I keep an updated list of all the various programs you can book with at MonkeyMiles.com/heres-a-list-of-every-hotels-vip-program-you-can-book/.

Here is the long and short of it.

When you book through a VIP program, you'll have the attention of the hotel manager; potentially get upgraded; get free breakfast, hotel credits, and bonus points; and, in many cases, get treated better than those who have elite status with the brand (and sunglasses inside are encouraged). OK, maybe not the last bit. But you are almost guaranteed to feel like an A-list celeb.

I always advocate comparing the VIP rates to others you may qualify for, like AAA (American Automobile Association), AARP, member rates, etc. When you're comparing, make sure you compare the checkout cost of the room rate itself. I consistently book these VIP rates because of the perks they include, which ultimately bring down the total checkout cost.

Let's wheel in the example.

On a whirlwind weekend trip to China, my wife and I stayed at the Peninsula Beijing booking through PenClub. PenClub is the Peninsula's VIP program. We booked the base room and received a free multicategory upgrade to a drop-dead gorgeous one-bedroom suite. We paid the same rate as the one advertised on the website but got that insane upgrade, free breakfast, and a property credit. If that wasn't enough, the hotel was made aware of our connection to the entertainment industry and made us a video camera out of dark chocolate as a welcome gift! Absolutely incredible. All because we used an adviser who was able to book us through PenClub. (Again, see the website on the previous page.)

The following brands all have VIP programs that you can access simply by contacting an adviser:

- Marriott
  - » Stars
  - » Luminous
- Hyatt
  - » Prive
- Hilton
  - » Impresario
- IHG
  - » Luxury and Lifestyle
- Belmond
  - » Bellini Club
- Dorchester
  - » Diamond Club
- Four Seasons
  - » Preferred Partner
- Mandarin Oriental
  - » Fan Club
- Oetker
  - » Pearl Partner

- Peninsula Hotels
  - » PenClub
- Preferred Hotels
  - » Platinum Partner
- Relais & Chateau
  - » Preferred Partner
- Rocco Forte
  - » Knights
- Rosewood Hotels
  - » Elite
- Sofitel
  - » STEP
- Shangri-La
  - » Luxury Circle
- Virtuoso
  - » Many hotels are individually a part of this program

Phew!

As you can see, there are maaaaaany ways to improve your travel, stretch your dollar, and unlock hidden perks and hacks. Heck, you can even be treated like an uber VIP without traveling a ton or using credit card points and miles!

My hope is that you're able to use bits and pieces of these tips and techniques to fine-tune your own version of being a savvy traveler, and focus your energy on the things you value most.

First Class Travel on a Budget

THE END

Wow! You made it.

Unless you're one of those people who can't help but skip to the last page to see how it ends. (Mom, I'm talking to you.)

Pat yourself on the back! You're officially ready to get out there and hack the trip of your dreams—wahoo!

I'm so grateful to you for reading this book, supporting me, and being a part of this journey that I never saw coming.

I had a plan to be a doctor, I had a plan to be an actor, but I never had a plan to travel the world with a stuffed monkey, write a blog, make educational and inspiring videos, and now publish a book.

Instead of following a plan, I followed my passion.

As you may have gathered, my heart is always yearning to figure out a deal, ideally one that enables me to take an aspirational trip and experience something new, exciting, and challenging. Everything I've learned and passed on to you in this book has been a result of listening to that little voice that said, "Just go for it." It's led me to incredible trips, career changes, and the love of my life. My hope is that you've felt a nudge to do as Bill Parrish advised in one of my favorite movies, *Meet Joe Black*, "Forget your head and listen to your heart. The truth is, there's no sense living your life without this." Hopefully I equipped your head with some education on credit and travel hacking, but more importantly, I hope you feel compelled to listen to your heart and step toward whatever road it yearns to pursue.

If you see me in an airport, on a plane, at a hotel, or taking a picture of Miles balanced precariously on one of the Wonders of the World, please do say hello! I'd love to hear what you're keeping in your wallet, where you've traveled, and what destinations are on your bucket list. Let's geek out together!

I always love hearing your impactful travel stories.

Traveling has been one of the most integral parts of my development as a person. Experiencing different cultures, meeting all kinds of people, and navigating the adventures that come with it all have opened my mind and heart. Traveling has transformed my life and continues to fuel my desire to explore and share how you can do it too! Thank you for being part of this incredible journey we're all on together!

Allow me to leave you with this: Secure your credit, tailor your wallet, and if you find yourself in a situation where you must lie, lie flat with your champagne held high.

God bless you in all your endeavors!

Zach and Miles :)

ACKNOWLEDGMENTS

To my mom and dad. You have given me the greatest gift of all: unconditional love. A gift so few truly experience and one that I am forever grateful to have received. You gave me the confidence to pursue my dreams, work hard, get back up, and no matter what, just "keep going." I always knew I had your unwavering support and whatever success I achieve in life is greatly a derivative of that knowledge. This book would have never happened without the tools you gave me and taught me to sharpen, and that I hope to one day give my children. I've been all over the world, but there is no place like home. I love you both so very, very much.

To my wife, Elizabeth. You've been my biggest champion, confidante, best friend, and a source of endless laughter and encouragement. You make every day better, and this book would never have happened without your daily affirmations and love. You've helped me build my business, create content, stay true to myself, and never jeopardize who I am in the process. Your soul is as much in these pages as mine. I love you to the moon (which one day we may visit on points).

To everyone at Page Street Publishing who made this book possible. It is no simple feat, and without Marissa Giambelluca, my editor, none of this would have been possible if you didn't reach out and take a chance on me. Never did I ever imagine I'd be a published author, and I have you to thank for this. To William, Meg, Rosie, Doreen, Laura, Jamie: Thank you for making my book so special!

(Continued)

To Dave Maurer. Who would have thought that all those years ago, being crammed into smelly hostels across Spain would forge an incredible bond never to be broken. We've literally been around the world more times than I can count, but the best part is just time spent together. Whether it be in an Argentinian speakeasy sipping cocktails, chuckling at lions mating in the wild, trying to keep warm in Jordanian martian tents, or simply having coffee at your house, it's always an adventure, and filled with moments I'll forever treasure. You've trusted me to load your wallet with credit cards and start trips without flights booked back home. You're the brother I never had, the one I can call about anything and everything, and your spirit is woven throughout this book.

To Daniella Giglio. You kept saying start a blog, start a blog, start a blog, and I'll never forget the kind words of affirmation and encouragement that kick started it all. God really does wink ;).

To Randy Petersen. To the man, the myth, the Godfather of points and miles, I could never fully express my gratitude for taking a chance on me as a blogger. It was a pivotal point in my travel career and one that I'm forever in your debt for. I needed some indication that I was on the right path, and it couldn't have come from someone whose professional opinion I valued more. I thank you from the bottom of my heart.

ABOUT THE AUTHOR

Successful entertainer and travel expert Zachary Burr Abel has amassed over 250 million social media views and over 1.5 million followers who smash the like button for his funny and informative videos focusing on credit tips, travel tricks, and "Zach hacks." If you're under 30 and carry an AARP membership, it's probably due to Zach's viral video that ended up getting AARP over 150k new members and landed Zach in the *Wall Street Journal*.

If you're thinking Zach looks familiar, you may recognize him from *90210*, *The Big Bang Theory*, *The Secret Life of the American Teenager*, and most famously for his series regular role on the hit show *Make It or Break It* where he played elite gymnast Carter. He put his acting career on hold at the end of 2014 when he chose to have spine surgery.

During a prolonged recovery and recuperation, he utilized his finance degree to launch his travel hacking website, Monkey Miles. Seven years, and over 2,500 articles later, it's the backbone of his business where he writes daily in-depth articles on credit cards, airline and hotel loyalty programs, and how to travel the world in luxury for pennies on the dollar. He flies over 100k miles a year, has earned and redeemed millions of points, visited 45 countries, 6 continents, carries 25+ credit cards, maintains an 800+ credit score, and has "Gotchu Baby!"

INDEX